YOUR GIANT OR YOUR MONSTER

Who Is Winning the Wealth Game?

How to Find the Inner Power to
Achieve More Success in Life and
Discover What is Holding You Back

Josue Lopez

Your Giant or Your Monster
Who is winning the wealth game?
How to find the inner power to achieve more success in life and discover what is holding you back

Copyright © 2019 Josue Lopez

ISBN: 978-1-939237-72-9

No part of this publication may be reproduced stored in a retrieval system or transmitted in any form or by any means electronic mechanical photocopying recording scanning or otherwise.

All rights reserved including the right to reproduce this book or portions thereof in any form whatsoever.

The information given in this book should not be treated as a substitute for professional medical advice; always consult a medical practitioner. Any use of information in this book is that of the readers discretion and risk. Neither the author nor the publisher can be held responsible for any loss, claim, or damage arising out of the use, or misuse of the suggestions made, the failure to take medical advice, or for any material on third party websites.

Published by
10-10-10 Publishing
Markham ON

Contents

Dedication	vii
Foreword	ix
Preface	xi
Acknowledgements	xiii
Chapter 1: Riches Revealed	**1**
Starting Life in the United States	3
A Fresh Start in Tampa, Florida	6
Chapter 2: Who Is Your Giant and What Is Your Monster?	**15**
The Story of the Two Wolves	15
The Monster Challenges the Giant	17
Awareness Is the First Step in Being Armed for Battle	18
A Choice Between Two Internal Powers	19
The Inner Giant	21
The Biggest Loser	25
It's Time to Choose	27
What Is Your Giant WHY?	30
Chapter 3: Your Purpose, Your Power	**35**
Why Is It Important to Have a Purpose?	35
Purpose and Mission	37
Clear and Specific Purpose	39
Having a Purpose Makes You Different	41
Become a Monster-Free Zone	42
Your Legacy Can Be Gigantic	44
How Do You Explain Life?	44
We Do Not Live Forever	47

Chapter 4: Creating the Future You Desire — 53
What Is a Goal? — 53
What Do People Think of the Goals? — 56
What Is the Difference Between a Goal and a Purpose? — 58
The Magic of Writing What You Want — 60
The Power of Visualization — 62
The Law of Attraction — 64
Are You Satisfied with Your Achievements? — 67

Chapter 5: What Is My Secret Formula? — 71
The Magic Pills — 71
The DKAR Formula — 73
Discipline — 74
Knowledge — 77
Taking Action Gets Your Mind in the Mood — 80
Results — 82

Chapter 6: What Tools Can You Use Right Now? — 87
The Power of the Mind — 87
Your Thoughts — 88
Your Belief System (BS) — 91
How Does the Mind Work? — 93
Ask Yourself Better Questions — 99
You Have Unlimited Power — 101

Chapter 7: What Is Your Giant's Code of Honor? — 107
Is Your Word a Contract? — 107
Can Other People Trust You? — 111
Are You a Person of Integrity? — 114
Are You Brave? — 116
Are You an Organized Person? — 118
Do You Help Others? — 121

Chapter 8: Can You Control What You Feel?   **127**
Fear: Is It Friend or Foe?   127
Can You Control Your Emotions?   130
What Is Your Definition of Failure?   132
Different Personalities   136
Do You Give 100% in Everything?   142

Chapter 9: Are You a Leader or a Follower?   **147**
How Do You Know if You Are a Good Leader?   147
Analyze Your Leadership Effectiveness   149
Self-Directed People Can Choose to Change—and Then Follow Through   150
Are You an Ordinary or Extraordinary Person?   151
The Things Great Leaders NEVER Do   155
Are You Winning the Big Game?   158
Are You a Determined and Persistent Person?   162

Chapter 10: What Are Your Beliefs About Money?   **167**
Is Money Good or Bad?   167
Some Say Money Is Not Important   168
Don't Blame Benjamin   169
Do You Know How to Listen?   170
Do You Like Change?   172
Is It Really That Simple to Achieve Financial Independence?   175
The Learning Habit   178
From Whom Do You Need to Learn, in Order to Have Money?   180

Chapter 11: Accepting the Gift	**185**
What Should You Do Now?	185
Don't Settle for Less Than Excellence	187
You Are Special	189
You, Without Limits	192
The Importance of Being Refined	196
Mission, Vision, Purpose, and Goals	198
What You Should Do Now	201
This Is Not a Dress Rehearsal for Life	204
About the Author	209

DEDICATION

To the two most precious people in my life, my wife, Keren, and son, Josue, for their never-ending love and encouragement in the realization of my goals and dreams.

FOREWORD

Congratulations! You have taken the first step. You want to learn how to not only aim higher, but also to succeed in creating a bigger future for yourself. This book is focused on helping you clear out a path to succeed in life, including but not limited to, becoming wealthy. You are closer than you realize to being able to dramatically change your life for the better.

As the late Dr. Martin Luther King, Jr. said, "You don't have to see the whole staircase, just take the first step." And here you are!

Do not underestimate your ability to learn from others, from Josue Lopez and Your Giant or Your Monster: Who is Winning the Game? You don't have to reinvent the wheel, just study what is proven to work as you begin your journey to financial independence. Now you have the opportunity to learn from Josue Lopez, a true hero in his own life.

He is a Cuban refugee who immigrated to the US when he was only 12. In this book you will hear about the incredible path that took him from being a near-starving child in Cuba to being a true success story as an American entrepreneur, husband, father, speaker, and philanthropist.

Whatever success means to you, after reading this book you will have a better understanding of yourself, and how your mind works. You will be able to identify two incredible powers that you possess inside: the "giant" and the "monster."

Your Giant or Your Monster: Who is Winning the Game? is a worthwhile read, and if you take what Josue teaches to heart and follow the suggested "Actions to take," you will achieve financial freedom, sooner than you may think. First, you must understand that the choice is yours— will you give control of your life to your inner giant?

Raymond Aaron
New York Times Bestselling Author

PREFACE

What does a poor, high school dropout, from a socialist state under communist rule, Cuba, have to teach about becoming rich, financially independent, and free?

You are about to find out. Precisely because I have such a unique background and a track record of overcoming major life challenges, you are going to find new concepts, advice, and specific actions to take, which will work for you like nothing you've ever tried before.

I have always wanted to help others get out of poverty and be on their way to financial freedom. I started fulfilling this life mission when I was in my twenties, and I started making enough money to help my many, many family members, including some who were stuck in the difficult conditions of today's Cuba.

My wife is my partner in my life mission, and together we have achieved everything we set out to accomplish. We still have big dreams, but for right now, my highest priority is to share what I've learned with anyone who has enough desire to learn exactly how to build wealth. This is one of the reasons why I wrote this book. It's all here. I've held nothing back, because life may take me in another direction once this book is published. I may not get a second chance to share all my secrets; who knows?

Reading this book has the potential to change your life forever. If you choose to study each distinction, starting with understanding your inner giant vs. your inner monster, you will have the foundation for becoming financially independent. If you also fully engage with the "Actions to take now" assignments at the end of each chapter, you will be well on your way to tremendous achievement. And by incorporating all the hard-won lessons in this book, you will reach your goal, if your desire is to become financially independent while having integrity, compassion, and love for others.

My wealth creation plan is all about balance, perseverance, and courage vs. fear. Anyone can follow it. Not many will choose that commitment, but since you are reading this, I have every hope for you. Trust the process, and after you read this book and start working your own plan, drop me a line. I'd love to hear about your own journey to financial freedom.

Josue Lopez
buildingyourgiant@gmail.com

ACKNOWLEDGEMENTS

Writing a book may seem to be an individual task, but the reality is that it is a team effort. First of all, I want to thank Keren Lopez, my beautiful wife for 16 years. You are my soul mate, the half that I was missing, and my best friend. Without your help, love, encouragement and efforts, this book couldn't have been written. I will love you forever.

Josue M Lopez, my son and my best friend, today, I'm a better man because of you. You inspire me to be all that I can be. Thank you for your support and for giving me so much love, joy, and happiness.

To my mother, Flor Lopez, for always believing in me and for being a stellar example of perseverance and love. I will always love you with all my heart.

To my father, Isaac Lopez, for making the decision to bring our family to the United States, in search of a better life. Without your courage, the door of opportunity would have remained closed.

To my sister, Sunny, for always giving me her unconditional love. Live your dreams!

With much appreciation and admiration, I acknowledge Raymond Aaron, a *New York Times* top 10 bestselling author and international motivational speaker. Thank you for your encouragement and help getting my book completed, and for contributing the foreword.

Barbara Dee is an editor, author of four books, and publishing partner to clients throughout the US. You have taken the quality of my book to a higher level through your editing. Thank you. I'm so grateful you believed in my dream, and helped me on my journey to become a published author.

Alejandro Victoria, my cousin, I want to thank you for your help and support, and for working with me in this project, with patience and passion.

I also want to thank the Caribbean Companies, LLC team, Eduardo Arriola, Armin Ferreras, and Enot Angles, for all their hard work and dedication to the business. Their commitment made it possible for me to dedicate the time to write and publish this book.

I am indebted to my Toastmasters Int'l club, Sarasota Speakers Exchange. I really want to thank all the members for providing a supportive learning environment, and helping me every week to improve and become a better speaker and trainer.

Finally, I'm grateful to all those that directly or indirectly contributed to my success by motivating me and guiding me in the right direction to finish this book.

Chapter 1

Riches Revealed

*"When your desire is ardent,
excuses and obstacles are overcome."
– Josue Lopez*

Every story has a beginning, and my family origins are in Cuba. In the middle of this island nation, in a small town named Sagua La Grande, in the province of Villa Clara, I lived with my family until I was 12 years old. It was an idyllic rural setting for a child to run free, exploring and learning the land and its inhabitants—horses, cows, goats, chickens, and pigs, along with wildlife, including, hutia, iguanas, and so many species of birds—all surrounded by a beautiful backdrop of mountains. I thought nothing of running up and down the mountains, and I would jump from the high elevations into the river below, facing my fears head on. When I look back on those times, it still sends a rush of adrenaline through me.

Being the adventurous child that I was, you can imagine how much I hated school. It wasn't the learning that bored me, but having to do it while sitting in a classroom chair for hours at a time. I felt tied down at school, and instead of teaching me discipline, it seemed to only fuel my wanderlust. There was so much in the outside world that I was eager and curious to explore.

At home, I was taught about God. My family was very religious, and I learned the importance of having a good relationship with our Creator. I also learned how to be grateful and respectful, and the value of hard work. I do not remember learning about money; I think it's because my family did not have much. There was no conversation about how poor we were, nor about how we could improve our circumstances by increasing our income. It was just the way it was. We gave thanks for what we had, and we got by as best we could with everyone pitching in to do the work that was in front of us.

I remember every time I told my father that I did not know how to do something, his answer was always the same: "Aprende, aprende, aprende." ("Learn, learn, learn.") Little did I realize at the time that those are magic words. That is, they appear so simple, yet work like powerful magic when applied in life.

When I was nine years old, I was in charge of my grandfather's wood charcoal business, as well as caring for our three horses, buying our daily bread, and going to different places to find and buy food. I was a very responsible child, and I always wanted to learn about how things worked, especially business. As hard as my family and I worked, we barely had money for necessities. In 1990, our circumstances got even worse. Due to governmental problems, the entire country of Cuba was going through a great economic crisis. Food was scarce. I remember eating nothing but boiled bananas, with no salt or oil, for a very long time. I learned what it was like to go to bed hungry.

Finally, my parents, my sister, and I had the opportunity to leave Cuba. My father paid a high price for this opportunity: a total of four years in prison. In Cuba, it is required by law that, upon turning 18 years of age, you are obligated to serve in El Servicio Militar Obligatorio (training in the army). There is no choice—either serve or end up in jail. My father's refusal to serve, as well as forgetting to show up for a government meeting, resulted in his incarceration.

What I learned from this experience is that you really never know why bad things happen. First, we don't want to accept when something bad happens; then we complain and feel terrible, but the reality is that we can always learn something from whatever happens, if we choose to. In this case, because my father went to jail, my parents, my sister, and I had the opportunity to come to the United States. His hardship proved worth it in the long run.

As I learned later, freedom of speech and religion, according to the Constitution of the United States of America, are basic human rights. The U.S. has a visa program for individuals who live in a country where their human rights are violated or they are politically persecuted. My father, among others, had been jailed because they were conscientious objectors who refused to join the Cuban Army. This made him and his immediate family eligible for the visa program. This is why we were able to legally come, by plane, to the United States, drastically changing the course of our lives forever.

Starting Life in the United States

We arrived in the U.S., in September of 1991, when I was 12 years old. We were welcomed at the airport by some friends of my parents. We did not have family in this country, nor money, but luckily, my parents were rich in friendship. Beatriz and Reynaldo Roques invited us into their home. We stayed with them for several weeks until we received some money from friends and were able to rent a small, studio apartment in Hialeah, Florida. Even at the age of 12, I knew that what they did for our family was a big sacrifice and responsibility, one I did not take for granted, and something that my family and I will always be grateful for. Nonetheless, the life of a person who immigrates to another country is very challenged. Living in Hialeah was especially difficult because we were not used to living in a city, and my parents could not find work. Eventually, we decided to move to Homestead, Florida.

In those years, Homestead was more like a country town and reminded us of our former small, rural town of Sagua La Grande. We loved it. I no longer had the mountains, but I was able to play in the street, and that suited me just fine. My parents started working, and I also found some odd jobs from time to time. In August of 1992, eleven months after arriving in the U.S., and just as we were beginning to adapt to our new lives, Hurricane Andrew stormed directly through Homestead, causing over $27 billion in damages, and leaving 65 people dead. It was a devastating time for our entire community, but we were alive, so we had to keep going.

My family did not lose much because we did not have much. Not having electricity, air conditioning, or a working stove was not a problem—that's how we had lived in Cuba. In fact, at times we felt like we were back there. After a few days, we started receiving donations, and from that moment on, we always had plenty of food and water. I helped to distribute many of the donated goods throughout the community. Once residents began repairing and rebuilding, I started working in roofing, making what I thought was a lot of money—$100 per day! I was only 13 years old, and my older, more experienced coworkers were earning the same as me. A fortunate opportunity for me had come from the bad event of the hurricane. After a few months, they finally fixed my school, which had been heavily damaged in the storm. I had no other choice but to quit my lucrative job and go back to spending my days stuck in a classroom.

I continued to look for and find work on the weekends and in the afternoons. There was something burning inside me that wanted to help my family get out of poverty. What I wanted for us was to live in a nice house on a spacious farm, and have a good car with air conditioning. I also yearned to have a lot of money to send to my extended family in Cuba, because I knew they continued to live in extreme poverty. For whatever reason, I always felt that I was the man in charge of changing my family's life forever, and this has always motivated me. Perhaps you feel that way too. With a strong desire to move forward financially and help others, I realized this was my main purpose; my **"why."**

Just as I had back in Cuba, at school I felt like I was doing nothing but wasting my time. At 15 years of age, after finishing ninth grade, I thought I had found a smarter way to spend my time. It started as a summer job where I was working as a helper, and I was making more money than my parents. When it was time to go back to high school to enter the tenth grade, I said to my father, "I do not want to go back to school and waste my time; I want to continue working." His response was simply, "Okay, make sure you keep your job." That was it. My father had also left school when he was young, and did not see the value in it.

His brother and sister, who had finished school and had careers, were earning less money than he earned in Cuba. I was ecstatic when he did not argue about my own plans to drop out of school, because I was sure that by the time I turned 24, I was going to be rich.

Today, I know that leaving high school was a very bad decision. I did not know how to properly write or speak English when I quit. I worked as a helper on a large property during the day, and at a Winn Dixie grocery store at night. After that, I started my first business, buying, fixing, and selling cars, and I became a mechanic, but I was not making a lot of money. I decided to try something else, and I got involved in a multi-level marketing company that sold vacuum cleaners. I learned that I was not a good salesman, at least in that business. A friend and I became partners in a business, installing alarms and audio equipment for cars, but we didn't make it either.

These early entrepreneurial ventures left me broke, and I ended up having to take a job as an electrician. I tried so many things, but nothing was earning me the money and success I desired. When I look back at those years, *I know that I was also experiencing many internal struggles*. A part of me had a **burning desire** to achieve big things and be financially successful, while another part of me doubted my ability to accomplish this, not believing I was good enough.

A Fresh Start in Tampa, Florida

Because I was working very hard but not getting rich, I blamed the city of Homestead and the people who lived there. I was desperate to move. Shortly after my sister had gotten married and moved to Tampa, Florida, my mother asked me if I, too, would be interested in moving there. I remember saying, "When do I start packing?"

Leaving my friends in Homestead, and once again starting over in a new city, was not easy, but it was a smoother transition than we had experienced coming to America from Cuba. I quickly found a job as an electrician and began saving money, with the intent to keep this particular job, at least until I turned 18.

As an electrician, I worked 10 to 14 hours a day to earn decent money, but again found myself with no riches to show for my hard work. In 1997, two weeks after turning 18, I quit my job and vowed that I would never again work for someone else. I was going to be the boss of me. I got my commercial driver's license and started working in the trucking business. With what little money I had saved, I purchased an old, beat-up truck for $6,000. The truck was green and reminded me of a giant avocado. I can honestly say that I probably had the worst truck in Tampa Bay, but I did not care. My sights were set on becoming my own boss and pursuing my goal of being rich, not on how good I looked getting there.

Unfortunately, I did not know then what I know now, and I did exactly what most people do when they become self-employed. I started working day and night, thinking that the secret to getting rich and becoming successful was to exchange my time for money, then more time for more money, and on and on. Following this method, I eventually got to a point where I was only sleeping a couple hours a day, for years, and barely took any breaks. Now I was exchanging my time and my health for money.

By the year 2000, I was not doing well. I was not yet rich, the balance in my life had completely disappeared, and I was not enjoying the process. In order to feel that there was at least some reward for my efforts, I bought my first house at the age of 21, in Riverview, Florida. Having a four-bedroom, two-bathroom home on a large lot in a nice area of town, was a great achievement— all my family moved in with me, but my life was still lacking something meaningful, something special.

Up to this point, I had spent so much time working hard that I had yet to have a girlfriend. I had never taken a real vacation, and I had racked up $21K in credit card debt, not to mention having the added expenses of now owning a home. I was feeling very frustrated with life.

Yet, incredible as it may sound, I was able to accomplish my goal of becoming rich at age 24— very, very rich. Now, you're probably thinking that I must have won the lottery, and in a way, I did. I was super lucky to meet and fall in love with an amazing, beautiful Cuban woman who, like me, had big goals and dreams. After struggling and sacrificing for so long, I found someone with whom to discover the beauty of life.

We got married, and on the first night of our honeymoon, we stayed in the largest room at the Don Cesar Hotel, on St. Pete Beach. From our large balcony, overlooking the gorgeous Gulf of Mexico, I literally felt like we were in a castle.

That night, after my queen fell asleep, I stood on the balcony gazing at the stars and the moon as they reflected on the ocean. Feeling like the king of the world, I said to myself, *After everything, if I can achieve this, from here on, I will be unstoppable*. Do you remember a day in your life when you felt unstoppable?

The next day, we embarked on a seven-day honeymoon cruise, and that was when I truly discovered that life is good—very, very good. Now, I knew my wife didn't marry me for money, because I didn't have any, but being alone with her on this cruise ship, the largest in the world at that time, was an out-of-this-world experience. The ship stopped in Labadee, Haiti; Ocho Rios, Jamaica; George Town, Grand Cayman and Cozumel, Mexico. The luxury of the cruise, the beautiful sites of the mountains and the islands, and the endless abundance of food and drinks made me feel that all the sacrifices I had made were worth it. Life was not only a great struggle, but it has a beautiful side, too, and it was up to me—us—to explore it. Then and there I promised my wife that every year we would take a real vacation—a vacation where we can enjoy life and the rich beauty of the world that surrounds us. I've kept that promise ever since.

It was around the year 2000 when I was first introduced to an audio tape by Anthony "Tony" Robbins, on which he talked about the kaizen philosophy, a Japanese term for "continual improvement." It is a principle which the Japanese, especially in industry, understand very well. Is it any wonder that the Japanese have had such global achievements and advancements in the past several decades? Constant and never-ending improvement can apply to all areas of life.

Now I ask you: Are you constantly improving yourself every day? If you are reading this book, the answer to that question is either a firm "yes," or you have at least challenged yourself to begin to improve, one step at a time. One thing is for sure, if you are not committed to constantly improving your life, you will continue to encounter many undesirable challenges, most of which you will not know how to solve. *Holding to the same attitudes and actions will produce the same outcomes, and to expect otherwise is foolish.* While *change* may seem hard, deciding to *improve* may be a less intimidating way to look at changes you must make in order to produce the outcomes you most desire.

Make the decision today to learn something new every day, and you will find the pressures of life begin to lift. Make sure you do not go to bed at night before learning something new and useful that you can use to improve your life and the lives of others. I always love to learn, and every day I learn something new.

When I look back now at my years of labor and struggle, I easily recognize why, although I was always working hard, nothing was paying off. You've probably noticed that my story revolved around always trying to make a lot of money. I worked hard at every job I had, but I never worked hard on myself. I had no one else to blame for my lack of monetary riches. I never learned business principles, I never learned how to build a company, and I never learned how to manage money. I was afraid to talk to people, and I did not know how to sell. I thought hard work would unlock the world's riches (especially in America!), but the key ingredients were missing in me, all along.

Remember, I've always felt it was my responsibility to make myself rich financially so I could help all the people I cared about get out of poverty. It wasn't until I invested in my own growth, and accepted that I needed to build myself before I could build a fortune, that I was truly granted the opportunity to help them.

Over the years, my parents and I have been able to help my family in Cuba by sending money, medicine, clothes, and other necessities to Cuba, most of the time sacrificing our own needs and wants. Stating in 2017, my wife and I have been able to help in a big way; all because we have become financially independent, and we are in a position where we can help even more. If you want to experience life the same way, I can tell you that it is possible, and you can do it, but nothing will change until you are willing to change—until you are willing to do something differently, until you are willing to learn, and until you are willing to grow personally.

Actions to take now:

We all have a story. Sit alone in a quiet place and, in a notebook or on your computer, begin to write yours. You do not have to write everything, but from your childhood until now, write the positive things that happened to you, the ones that stand out the most. The negative things that happened to you will also come to mind, so focus on the ones that taught you the most, the ones that taught you to be a better person. **You first have to know where you are, then you can figure out where you are going**. Your story can reveal rich lessons, insights, and proof of improvements. Remember, we are here creating a story in which we are the main character. How is your story going?

Notes

Chapter 2

Who Is Your Giant and What Is Your Monster?

"When the battle is eternal, you must always be alert."
– Josue Lopez

The Story of the Two Wolves

In this fable, a Cherokee Indian grandfather is teaching his grandson about life. He tells him: "There is a fight inside me. It's a terrible fight, and this fight is between two wolves. One is bad—it represents anger, envy, pain, grief, greed, arrogance, self-pity, guilt, resentment, inferiority, lies, false pride, superiority, and ego."

After a time, he continued, "The other wolf is good—it is joy, peace, love, hope, serenity, humility, kindness, benevolence, empathy, generosity, truth, compassion, and faith. The same struggle is happening within you, and within all people."

The grandson was quiet for a minute and then asked his grandfather, "Which wolf will win?"

The old Cherokee replied, "The one you feed."

I was drawn to this story when I first heard it, because I could identify with it. All of my life, I've had an internal fight between two conflicting powers, although I would not necessarily characterize them as *good* and *bad*. Universally, we can understand the fable about the wolves, about good vs. evil, but my inner fights have been a bit different. Many of them have not been so great, but some of these fights were terrible battles. A few have lasted for years at a time, and in some of them, I hated the winner. In my case, it is not only the struggle between good and evil; rather, the biggest struggles for me have been between what I want in life and what I think I am capable of achieving.

I believe almost all of us are fighting this inner battle. For example, we want to have a kind, intelligent, attractive mate, but we do not think we can find one because we don't think we are attractive enough ourselves. We want to be physically fit, but we do not think we have the time or money that it takes to eat healthy and workout. We want to have a nice, big house with a pool, and have it paid off, but we think that it would take a lifetime to accomplish. We want to have more money, but we think that we are not smart or good enough to have a lot of it.

It is not hard to uncover these conflicting thoughts when you talk with someone about their life, goals, or dreams, no matter what that person's age, gender, or education. I've heard countless examples, especially about money. We want to be promoted at work, but we think we'll be passed over for someone fresh out of college. We want to own our own businesses, but we do not think we have a skill or product worth selling. We want to achieve financial independence so that we never have to worry about money again, but we think it is only possible if we win the lottery. We are constantly having thoughts that tell us we cannot have what we want. And we believe them!

The Monster Challenges the Giant

When I shared this story of two wolves with my son, I put my own spin on it. I said to him, "There is a fight inside of me. It's a terrible fight, and the fight is between a giant and a monster. The monster is full of fear, doubt, indecision, negativity, and lacks faith. In some ways, he is a monster, but really, he is just a big chicken. And he is lazy, undisciplined, and weak, and has a bad attitude. Because he is so disorganized, he never feels prepared, capable, or confident. He believes he will never succeed since he is not intelligent nor good enough."

My son was nine years old at the time, and I could tell that his imagination was reeling with what probably looked like a cross between a scary alien monster and a half-dead chicken—ugly, with no redeeming qualities, for sure. I had his attention, at least.

I continued: "The giant is strong, he is fearless, he has a positive attitude, he is disciplined, he is brave, and he encourages others. He is willing to leave his comfort zone, and he is capable of achieving great things. Can you picture this giant?"

My son nodded yes, and interestingly, his demeanor and body language had changed—he sat tall and leaned toward me, eager to hear more about this *super hero* I was describing.

"The giant within me enjoys helping others and has a strong faith. He is organized and decisive, and he believes in himself. He knows he is intelligent, and he feels prepared to achieve success in every aspect of life. He knows he is good enough to accomplish all that he wants in life. He is unstoppable."

I waited a few moments for my son to absorb all I had said about the monster and the giant within me. Then I looked squarely into his eyes and said, "The same fight is happening within you. This battle rages within every man and woman on planet Earth. It's part of what it means to be human."

Then I asked my son, "Do you know who wins this fight inside of me every day?"

"No," he said.

"Look at my actions and you will find out."

Awareness Is the First Step in Being Armed for Battle

For many people, making the decision to do the right thing or the wrong thing, every day, is the biggest dilemma. And for others, like me, finding the inner power to achieve what we want in life is the biggest challenge. The first step, as in much of life, is to become aware. How would you describe your *two wolves?* At times, an internal battle can feel like a whole pack of wolves are involved—yes? You also must be aware of the fact that you get to decide which comes out the winner. I wrote this book out of my commitment to share my experience, understanding, and my secrets about how to access the internal power that we all have. Stick with me, and you will learn how to take control of your life by awakening the giant and leaving the monster lying dormant inside of you.

Who Is Your Giant and What Is Your Monster?

A Choice Between Two Internal Powers

Nothing impresses me more than my fellow human beings. I am awed by all the good things they do, and also the bad. By paying close attention to mankind's actions, one can easily see that we have incredible power. We have the power to make this world a perfect place to live, and we also have the power to destroy it. The power exists; we just have to make the decision to use it in the right ways.

What if we could truly choose our battles? Imagine how different this world would be if we did not have to spend more resources on armament and troops for war. Imagine using all that money, all that technology, all those intelligent minds who are constantly preparing for war, to instead seek solutions to the great problems of humanity, such as hunger and diseases.

If all of these people were to focus on balancing the world and educating humans to improve their lives and become better people, we could make the world a profoundly better place to live in just a short time.

Does a voice inside you dismiss that vision with cynicism? *That's a good dream but will never happen*, the monster says. If there is anything I have come to believe from firsthand experience and hard evidence, it is that many good dreams come true.

Look around at all of the good we see in the world today. Gaze upon the beauty of our planet, and at the amazing achievements mankind has made to enrich our lives. Now it is up to us to repeat more of the good. Most of the time we expect other people to change the world, or we have the mentality that only God can do it. I believe that God can change the world through each person, and that person can be you.

When you strive to be the best person that you can be, you will not only live a beautiful life but, more importantly, impact the world in a positive way to improve it. This struggle to conquer the internal monster and use one's innate power for good is unique to mankind. When we look at the whole of mankind and all the turmoil in the world, the battle can appear complex and overwhelming. Don't look there. Look in the mirror. Past U.S. President, Theodore Roosevelt, made this point in these often-quoted words: *"Do what you can, with what you have, where you are."*

It all comes back to the personal internal conflict that we all have between the giant and the monster. By design, neither the monster nor the giant can be destroyed. For as long as you live, so too will they. The giant can empower you to live the life you dream and desire, a life full of peace, abundance, and happiness; the monster will keep you trapped in a life of suffering.

While both powers exist, the monster that I am referring to lives only in your mind, while the giant resides in the beautiful mansion that is your heart. What I call your *monster* is that negative part of your mind that constantly generates limiting thoughts, doubts, disbelief, worries, fears, and barriers. It doesn't let you see things the way they really are, as it lives in your mind and clouds your thoughts and vision.

When you think about all the good things you want to accomplish, the things you would like to do for yourself, your family, and for other people, where does all that goodness come from? You bet; it is from your heart, not your mind. Just as your mind's monster generates negative energy, the giant who lives in your heart generates positive energy. And now that you have this crucial distinction, you know the truth. All that negative BS (Belief System) in your head is NOT WHO YOU ARE. Follow your heart, letting your giant guide you. Your giant will always know what is best for you. The work that lies ahead for you is to learn to trust him.

You have everything you need inside you to create the life you want, but you have to use your inner power to become more, not only because you will live a richer life both personally and professionally, but because you can help others do the same. Life is very valuable and wonderful, so let your giant take control of it, and he will take you where you want to go, and beyond.

Many of us do not take time to consider or meditate on these two internal powers. We feel them, but we do not understand them, and we do not know how to explain or manipulate them. *On a daily basis, we are dealing with an inner battle, and yet we do not realize what is happening to us*. That's why many give up and simply focus on survival, instead of focusing on creating a better life and helping others along the way. Let's really focus on this internal battle, and understand everything we can about it. As we often hear, knowledge is power.

The Inner Giant

Why do I believe that what we have inside is a giant? Imagine the good things that millions of people have done for humanity, or perhaps, for you. There are many people who have not allowed their inner monster to take control of their lives. If you study the lives of very successful people, you will discover that they have harnessed the power of their inner giant in order to accomplish extraordinary, constructive things. Many of these people have impacted my life in a very positive way. It is amazing how many times the highest achievers will say something like, "I came from humble beginnings. If I can do this, you can, too." I choose to believe them, and you can choose to believe this for yourself, too.

What makes all these people extraordinary is that they are willing to do something that most people are not willing to do, and they have a better understanding of the ways in which their mind works. The reality is that we all have the potential to be extraordinary human beings. *We already have what we need inside of us to not only build a successful life for ourselves but to make positive and important changes in the world.* We simply have to be willing and able to follow through with our burning desire and do what is good and right.

Yes, it usually feels easier to just create excuses and avoid possibly paying the price for risks we must take, despite the potential for reward. However, if you commit to work on yourself, and follow the steps you are about to learn in this book, I know that your giant will take control and, after you understand how your mind works, you too will be extraordinary.

Now I have a question: Will you be a part of the disciplined group that will devote time and effort to discover your full potential? Are you going to believe in you? You have what you need to get ahead—you just have to do things differently than you've ever done them. Before you answer my question, let me give you some examples so you can more fully understand your own giant and monster.

A few examples:

It is 5:00 in the morning, and your alarm tells you it is time to get up so you can get to the gym before work, but your mind is swirling in justifications for hitting *snooze* and remaining in your warm, comfortable bed. You hear: Don't get up now; you need more rest. You can go to the gym after work. (YOUR MONSTER)

Listen again as the soft voice tells you to stick to your plan so you can stay healthy, strong, fit, and energized. (YOUR GIANT)

You arrive home after a long day at the office, and a part of you wants only to sit in front of the TV for three hours, tune out, and do nothing. (YOUR MONSTER)

But listen carefully, and you will hear another voice that says: Pick up the personal development book you started reading last week. Remember how inspired and motivated it made you feel. You have time right now, so use it wisely, and you will learn things that will make your life easier. (YOUR GIANT)

When it's time to eat dinner, your mind (and your stomach) is encouraging you to eat three plates of food, despite having eaten sensibly all day and working out at the gym as part of your goal to lose 20 pounds, as your doctor recommended. (YOUR MONSTER)

Listen again, and you will hear another voice encouraging you to stick to your healthy habits, reminding you that a small plate of food is enough to keep your body nourished and healthy. (YOUR GIANT)

It's finally the weekend. All week, you had planned to spend time cleaning the house and organizing your garage, but now you are thinking that you want to just lounge by the pool, and maybe take a nap. (YOUR MONSTER)

Listening for the voice behind that slacker, you can, if you try, hear the reminder that you will feel really good once the house and garage are handled, and then you can truly enjoy relaxing by the pool. (YOUR GIANT)

You come up with a great business idea, but in your mind, you are not intelligent enough; you do not have a college degree; you were born poor and you will always be poor; you can't be successful because of where you live; you don't have the nerve; you don't have the slightest idea how to double your income, and you don't think you could learn how; you are not good enough, anyway; you don't deserve it. (YOUR MONSTER)

But as you learn to tune in to the other voice inside you, you can hear the declaration that you can accomplish anything you desire; you can have courage, and face your fears, and you can learn new things. This voice comes from your mind and your heart, and tells you that if you are disciplined and choose every day to learn new and important things in order to achieve what you want, you can and you will achieve them. (YOUR GIANT)

The Biggest Loser

Why do I believe that what we have inside is also a monster? Just think for a minute. Think of the horrible things you've seen humans do. Think of terrorism, and the human beings that choose to strap bombs to their bodies in order to kill groups of innocent people. Think about what some humans have done to their own families and their own children. Some have opened fired at schools, banks, and nightclubs for no logical reason except to spread hatred and violence. Yes, sadly, people do terrible things to others every day. *When the monster wins, everyone loses.*

Think, also, about what people do to themselves. It is estimated that 160 million Americans are obese or overweight, according to www.healthdata.org. But we do not have to look for any statistics to recognize that this is a significant problem in both the United States and other parts of the developed world. Many argue that processed food is to blame, as well as all of the sugary beverages available to us from a young age. I do not disagree with this argument, but I wonder, *why are there other people who live in the same environments, who are not overweight?*

A large factor, I believe, is that these people have better control— of themselves, of their minds, and of what and how much they choose to consume. Others with less self-control will eat excessively and do little to no exercise to burn off any of the empty calories they are taking in. In fact, I'd be willing to bet that getting healthy and fit is important to them, but unfortunately, they don't have the discipline to follow thru. When I see someone, who is struggling with obesity, it shows me that they are also struggling with, and being controlled by, his or her own inner monster. If you can identify with this lack of self-control, know that what you will learn in this book will help you get your hands back on the controls that steer your life in the direction you want.

Another area in which our inner monster rules over us is with addiction, and I'm not even talking about drug addiction. Just look at the number of people who are addicted to smoking. Approximately 37.8 million adults in the United States currently smoke cigarettes, and 15 million people have problems with alcoholism. People may not always talk about it, but often times the addiction develops because someone is unhappy with life, and they attempt to mask the pain with harmful substances. They do not believe they can change themselves or their circumstances; they do not believe they can have a much better life. The pain and unhappiness continue, and so too does the addiction.

The negative belief that we are incapable of being extraordinary affects us all, and it starts when we are young. I recently had the privilege of speaking at a middle school. I asked the children, all between the ages of 11 and 14, "How many of you believe that you will finish this school year with straight A's in all your classes?" Only 5% raised their hands. Therein lies the problem: If they do not believe they can achieve something, there is no way they will. The super successful American business tycoon, Henry Ford, put it this way: *"Whether you believe you can do a thing or not, you are right."*

Adults also have very limiting beliefs. We do not believe that we can achieve greatness and, therefore, continue to fall short of reaching our unlimited potential. Each time we quit/fail, our inner monster wins—not because we are incapable of success, but

Who Is Your Giant and What Is Your Monster?

because we do not believe enough in ourselves to see it happen. This monster that we each possess is so powerful that it controls most people on a daily basis. It is the reason why most never discover their full potential.

You can continue to let your monster control you; that is exactly what he wants you to do. Or you can decide to take control. Fortunately, you have an inner giant that can help you do it. You can't change the past, but you can ensure a better future for yourself and those around you, starting today—starting now, in this moment.

First, you have to look at your *belief system*, and you have to be willing to do things differently in order to obtain different—better—results. Helping you get the life of your dreams is one of the reasons why I wrote this book. I don't spend a lot of time questioning why I feel called to communicate what I've learned; I just find that doors of opportunity keep opening for me to follow my passion. I speak to groups of all ages, I lead weekend workshops, and I've devoted myself to writing this book instead of a million other ways I could have spent my *free time. It is my privilege and passion to share what I am confident can be life-changing for you.*

It's Time to Choose

If you commit to reading this book completely, and following the steps within it, your giant will take control of your life forever. If you work on yourself and decide today to change your life, in a short period of time you will achieve what you want. But first, you must choose: Will you continue to let your monster hold all the power, or will you give control to your giant? Do not make this decision in haste. It is possibly one of the most important decisions of your life.

The path you choose today will determine what your life will be like in both the present and in the future. Every action you take will bring you closer to or take you further away from the important things you want to achieve or obtain during the remainder of your lifetime. Why put off any longer the life you want to live? Here is how one Spanish philosopher expressed this:

> "We cannot put off living until we are ready. The most salient characteristic of life is its coerciveness—it is always urgent, here and now, without any possible postponement. Life is fired at us point-blank."
> – Jose Ortega

If you still believe that this decision is not both important and urgent, I guarantee that your inner monster is in control. Think about how this decision may harm you or benefit you in your own life, but also think about the effect it can have on those around you. Do your parents live as comfortably as you would like them to live, or would you like them to have more security? What about your spouse or your children? Would you like to have more time for them and give them more of what this world has to offer? Think of your friends, and think of people you have never met. We do not realize the impact that each decision we make has on us and others.

Even one action you take can have a profound ripple effect. This means that, like ripples expanding across the water when a pebble is dropped into it, an effect from an initial action can be followed outwards, reaching far and wide.

When the monster is in control, we are blind to this. In truth, everyone on this planet has the potential to benefit from the decision you make today.

Life is valuable and should not be wasted. You were chosen to be put on this planet, and you have a responsibility to discover *why*, and to reach your maximum potential. Everything you need in order to do this is inside of you, but most people do not know it, and if you tell them, they do not believe it. Everything you want is within your reach. I repeat—everything you want is within your reach.

If you tell me you need more peace in your life, this is the first thing you will receive. More happiness? You will have it in abundance. You want to change your profession, or have your own business, or write a book, speak in public, impact large numbers of people with your own philosophy? You can do that, too! How about earn enough money to feel free and be able to do all the things you want in life? When you decide to let your giant guide you, that very day your life will change.

As soon as you choose to give control of your life to your giant, it is your responsibility to provide him with the necessary tools to nurture and strengthen him. In the next chapters, you will learn how to use the primary tools you will need, so your giant can be invincible.

What Is Your Giant WHY?

If you made the right decision, then starting today, your giant controls you. But there is something else that should be clear. You must know your reason *why*. We all have a different why. It is that which motivates you the most. For example, some people want to have more time for themselves and for their family. Others want to travel the world and experience life outside of their day to day routine. For some, the why is because they want to have more money in order to get out of poverty and achieve financial freedom. Or perhaps others want to cure a disease to make this world a better place to live in.

> *"All the great organizations in the world, all have a sense of why that organization does what it does."*
> – Simon Sinek

If you've been paying attention, you probably already know my why, but I'll share it with you again, now that you better understand what I mean. After coming to the United States from Cuba, where my large family and I were extremely poor in the material sense, I always felt it was my responsibility to help my family get out of poverty, not only the close family members with me in America, but also the ones I left behind in Cuba.

Every day, I worked hard, not only to improve my life and achieve all the things I wanted to achieve, but also because I'm motivated to provide a better life for my loved ones. **This is my biggest why.** By the time I turned 38 years old, I had achieved many of the goals I made for myself. All my life, I have been helping my family as best as I could, but only in the past few years have I been able to help in a more meaningful way, because I made the decision to let my giant be in control of my life.

With each day, I have more time and resources to give them, but it took a lot of learning to reach this point. For example, I've learned that most people do not know much about money, including my family. *The reality is that money problems cannot be solved with more money.* This goes against what most of us want to believe, but more often than not, when a person is living in poverty, it is because of the mindset they have about money. Living paycheck to paycheck is all they know, and it is a vicious cycle that is difficult to break away from. If you don't have a lot of money, the first thing you have to learn is to **manage** what you have, precisely, and keep these three things in mind: 1- Get the money. 2- Keep the money. 3- Multiply it. This is how you can solve money problems. Chapter 10 is all about money; just be patient.

Learn about investing your money. Learn how to make your money work for you. Up to this point, your monster has probably made you fearful of the risk of investing money that you feel you need to have it readily available to you. Remember, because you said so, your giant is in control now. And, if you haven't been satisfied with the results your monster led you to when it came to money, what better time than now to learn to trust your giant, do things differently, and see results that better align with your goals?

To win in the game of life, the number one rule is to know your *why*. To achieve success, you may have to do some things that you have been trying to avoid out of fear, laziness, or a lack of self-worth, but in your why is where you will find the motivation to continue improving and working on yourself every day. Answering the question of why may sound simplistic, but it is one of the most profound questions you could ever ask.

Who Is Your Giant and What Is Your Monster?

Actions to take now:

The first step to take, now that you've decided to let your giant take control, is to clearly state your **why**. Sit in a quiet place, focus your mind within, find your giant, talk to him, and ask him: What do you really **want** in life, and for what **reason**? Be still and listen. Write down what is in your heart and mind about your **WHY**. Even if you don't have this crystallized yet, start writing your thoughts as they are forming.

Then make a promise to your giant, a vow that has every fiber of your being behind it—tell your giant that starting today, he will have all the control over you. Promise yourself to be unstoppable. An equally important step to take right now: Tell your monster that his days are over, and that he has lost control over you. Adiós!

Your Giant or Your Monster

Notes

Chapter 3

Your Purpose, Your Power

"Efforts and courage are not enough without purpose and direction."
– John F Kennedy

Why Is It Important to Have a Purpose?

When you hear the word, *purpose*, what is the first thing that comes to mind? What is your definition of purpose at this very moment? The definition of purpose is: the *reason* why something is done or created or for which something exists. You might set up goals to reach a purpose related to personal development, a cure for a disease, or financial freedom. Of course, some people believe their purpose is to do evil, by inflicting harm on or killing innocent people, but we do not want to focus on those purposes, only the ones that will make your life, and the lives of others, better. There are many writings by wise people who have contemplated life and its purpose, and this is because it is a universally important inquiry for each person, even for you.

Do you think it is necessary to have a purpose in life? I have always believed that having a purpose in life is essential, but when I researched this topic, I realized that some do not believe that having and living with a purpose is a good idea at all. The explanation they give is that many people, get very focused to achieve something and they make great sacrifices for many years in order to achieve it, but do not enjoy life along the way. Their tunnel vision drives them to focus too narrowly, and they miss out on the vast opportunities life has to offer.

Another downside mentioned about living with a purpose is that once you fulfill that which you strived so long and intently for, you are overcome by a feeling of emptiness. There is nothing else to work toward. It's like how, in many cases, people who have achieved great economic success end up asking themselves: Is this all there is?

Living with a purpose does have its risks. It seems that part of human nature is that it is difficult for us to maintain balance in life. Imagine a mountain top. Our purpose is positioned at the apex of that mountain, and we want to reach it as quickly as possible. As we set out on our climb, sometimes we lose our balance and we stumble. We then become hyper-focused on not falling off the path to our purpose, and we forget to enjoy the view as we make our ascent. *It is important to remember that life is lived during the climb itself.*

There are always obstacles to face along the path. How we meet them is what shapes us as a person. Reaching our purpose at the top of the mountain is important, but we must maintain our balance along the way, or we are sure to fall off. Don't let the challenges unsettle you; instead, let them occur for you as simply a detour to the top. Maybe that detour will take you on an even more beautiful path, with an even better view.

Without the mountaintop to strive for, it is easy to give up and turn around when we hit an obstacle. With no compelling reason to climb on, we settle for what is more convenient and comfortable. With no purpose, it doesn't seem to matter if a detour runs us around in circles. If you don't have a good purpose in mind, you will not grow as a person, you will not reach your maximum potential, and you will never see the view from the top.

People who live life with a purpose have core beliefs and values that influence their decisions, shape their day to day actions, and determine their short- and long-term priorities. They place significant value in being a person of high integrity and in earning the trust and respect of others. They achieve balance and put their hearts into their journey and into building relationships with friends and families. They also do more for their country and for humanity. These people always have many reasons to feel powerful.

Many experts believe, as I do, in that to win big in the game of life, having a clear purpose will help you achieve all your goals and dreams a lot faster. Your inner giant thrives when you have a clear purpose. Your giant within needs clarity about what direction to go, and why.

Purpose and Mission

Purpose is usually distinguished as different from a mission. When we read or hear about a mission, it is defined or described as being an important assignment carried out for political, religious, or commercial purposes, typically involving travel. An astronaut has a mission; an evangelist heading to another continent to start a church has a mission; a marketing manager who is tasked with getting a new brand known nationwide has a mission. Now when I hear people talking about **life** purpose or **life** mission, I believe they are talking about the same thing. If the word, *life,* is in front of purpose or mission, we are talking about essentially the same thing.

Let me explain the way I see it. I will always work hard to accomplish my purpose, whatever it may be. Now, I don't have a life purpose; what I have is a **life mission,** and it should be such that it will continue to have an impact, even after my days on this earth are through. For example, my life mission is this: **"To eliminate poverty from people's minds and their lives."** The first thing I did was eliminate poverty from my own mind. By doing this, I was able to eliminate poverty from my life. Now I'm working hard to eliminate poverty from the lives of my family. Once I can say that I've accomplished that, I will continue helping others.

I know, in my lifetime, I will not eliminate the poverty of every single person in the world, but by the time I leave this planet, I know I will have impacted the lives of millions. I will have helped to make a difference, and others will continue with this mission. The purposes in my life will lead me to achieving my life mission, and that is why you must always work hard to accomplish them. Keeping them clear and at the forefront of your mind will help you do just that.

Clarity of purpose can energize everything you do. Your giant thrives when you have a purpose and a life mission. These are the incentives you need in order to feel alive. When the giant begins each day with a purpose in mind, it is easy to find the energy, the desire and the power to perform any necessary task that brings him closer to fulfilling it. At this moment, you may not yet know exactly what your life mission is. In truth, this is the case for many people, but I am going to help you figure it out. Sure, there are people who know from a very young age what they want. Perhaps they know that they are destined to be singers or great athletes. My wife always knew that she would be an accountant. That is her profession today, and she loves helping others in that particular way. There are people who have great gifts and wonderful abilities, who know their purpose and their life mission, but we are not all like that.

In my case, until I turned 38 years of age, I didn't know what my life mission would be, but that did not prevent me from always trying to achieve my goals and from having a clear purpose. To get out of poverty, to have my own business, to become financially independent, for everything that I was doing, I had a purpose in mind, or a very good reason. Living with purpose, going after these kinds of achievements, supported and prepared me to discover my **life mission.**

Clear and Specific Purpose

Undoubtedly, there are some things that are bigger, more important, and more difficult to accomplish than others. We are the ones who have the opportunity to decide which one of them we will give priority to. In my case, taking care of my mind and body is one of my top priorities. I like meditation, working out and eating healthy – for example instead of focusing on what I should not eat, I find it easy to eat nutritious and delicious food as fuel for my body.

Your Giant or Your Monster

A friend told me to think about how a flight attendant, when addressing passengers on a plane, always says that if, in case of emergency, the oxygen mask from over the seat drops down, to be sure and secure your own mask on your face first, before assisting someone next to you. We all must learn that it is not selfish to practice self-care because it's actually one of the best ways to be able to help others as well.

Now think about this question, what is the point of achieving wonderful things if you do not have the health afterwards to enjoy them? This is the reason that motivates me to make the correct daily choices. I need a well-nourished, strong body to get me to the mountaintop!

If you want to have your own business, help the poor, become financially independent, etc. What's your specific purpose, what is your reason? If you start your business and your main reason is to make money and become wealthy, this might not be the best purpose. If you purpose is to solve a problem for people and get rich doing it, then you are on the right track.

If you want to help the poor, because you want to give back, or because you want to leave the world better than you found it, those are good reasons. Keep something in mind, *the best way to help the poor is by not being one of them.* Exactly like the example of putting your own oxygen mask first, you should focus first on getting yourself out of poverty.

If you want to be financially independent because you want to watch TV, or because you want to play video games all day, every day. This might not be a big enough purpose. If the reason is to have more time to spend with your family, or to work on your life mission, or to have the feeling that you never have to worry about money again, these are much better reasons.

Maybe your purpose is to go beyond being financially free. Your purpose could be to become extremely wealthy, given the opportunities in the world we live in today, we should all strive to become millionaires - without taking advantage of other people. In the year 2000, I met several people who had already amassed quite a bit of wealth. One of these was Guy Shashaty, a senior national sales director with Primerica. During a business meeting, he looked at me and said these words that I will never forget: *"Money will only make you more of what you already are. If you are bad in your heart, money is going to make you worse. If you are good in your heart, money is going to make you better."*

If you are a good person with a lot of money, you could choose to do wonderful things for others with the resources available to you. The more money you have, the bigger impact you can make, if that is your purpose. But first, in order to reach this level of success and wealth, it is important that you keep your purpose very clear. **Clarity gives you power**. When you have a clear, specific purpose, then you set goals, or put together a plan, or use a system to take massive action.

Having a Purpose Makes You Different

When I got married, at the age of 24, my wife and I made a financial plan, and the company that we used was Primerica Financial Service. We wanted to know our debt freedom date and the amount of money it would take to be financially free. For us, this was one of our most important priorities , and it was extra special because we shared it. We created, in writing, our blueprint to follow in order to achieve financial freedom. It took us 14 years to achieve our financial independence, but today we live as we want to live, without having to worry about money. Achieving this, for many people, seems impossible, but I want you to know that it is not. You just have to make the decision and commit to be free, and then be different from the majority of people who unfortunately will live life in a way that proves to themselves that financial freedom is impossible for them.

Today, my wife and I are working hard to be millionaires and we have a really good reason. When I share this goal with people, many are surprised. Because it seems like such an impossible feat to them, they think we must be crazy. Their monster still runs the show, so achieving wealth is believed to be out of reach and only for those who know some secret, or have some key that they do not possess.

In reality, all of the secrets of wealth have already been revealed; they are available to everyone. Even if you have heard the best advice in the world from a self-made billionaire, you have to create your own path to financial success. In this book, I not only explain many of these secrets, I will teach you how to train your inner giant to help you achieve everything you want for your own life.

Become a Monster-Free Zone

As you read and learn, you must keep in mind that in many cases, the people that surround us, like our partners, families, friends, co-workers, etc., hold us back. Negativity is very heavy. It will be much harder for you to get out of poverty, or achieve great things, if you are carrying the weight of the people in your life who are still being controlled by their monster. You are led by your giant, but they are controlled by their own monster, and monsters recruit monsters. They will try to keep you at the same place where their belief hit a brick wall.

They may discourage you and tell you that what you want to accomplish is impossible—that you do not have the experience, that you are not smart enough, that there is a lot of competition in the world, that the economy is too weak, or that you are too old, or too young. Often, they don't do this out of malice or to knowingly hold you back; rather, they do it out of their own fear of failure. They do not believe that the success you seek is possible, and they do not want you to suffer the disappointment that they believe is inevitable. If you are committed to your purposes and your life mission, you must stay away from these negative influences. They may think they are protecting you, but really, all they are doing is trying to weigh down your giant. You must protect yourself, and your giant, from them.

If they do not change their mindsets, negative people will never be satisfied with their achievements. They will live their lives dwelling on the past, while dreaming of winning the lottery. Their own monster has total control over them. Today, you are guided by your giant, and giants recruit giants. Partner with successful people so you can learn from them. Something that is difficult for everyone to accept is this: If you cannot change the people around you, change the people you are around. You may not have taken time before to consider whether each person you spend time with has their monster or their giant in control. Once you think about it, you'll see it. You must take steps to become a monster-free zone. You have to make radical decisions in order to live a wonderful life. If you want to win the game, another important rule to follow is that you have to be different in order to get a different result.

Your Legacy Can Be Gigantic

What are you working for? What do you want to achieve before your days on Earth are over? What will your legacy be? Because you are unique—there has never been a *you* before, and there never will be again—when you fully express yourself, you will be more special, leading an extraordinary life. That is what is possible when your giant is in control. Write a unique story, explore every single part of life and this planet. Make a difference in other people's lives, and you will be remembered as someone that left this world better than you found it. To do all of this, you must keep your promise to your giant, let him lead your life, and put yourself around other people with the same mindset.

How Do You Explain Life?

Life is the most wonderful thing there is to explore. We are deeply affected when someone close to us loses their life. Sometimes we feel the loss even if we have never met the person. Given that, you'd think that more people would appreciate the value of their own lives, but more and more, we see people all over the world who do not take care of themselves. I may not know you personally, but I can tell you about your giant. Your giant appreciates life and knows how valuable it is. To your giant, life is about truly living life to its full potential. Life is about thriving, not just surviving.

For your monster, on the other hand, life consists only of temporary satisfactions. Your monster only wants to survive. He wants to avoid all kinds of risks. He loves to waste every precious day with trivial pursuits. The monster just wants to get by, living a life with no purpose, hoping to win the lottery as the only solution to all his problems.

When we reflect on our lives, we may realize that our own emotions and beliefs have become more important than life itself. These thoughts, feelings, and beliefs about what life should be, sometimes drown out our ability to recognize the positive things that are occurring in our lives as they are. Especially with social media and people having the ability to portray their lives to others as something that they are not, the pressures to be perfect are far-reaching. Unfortunately, the weight can be too much for some to bear, and they choose to take drugs or find other ways to numb their feelings. Some even decide to give up, to end their lives. Understand that if you are reading this book, you have a life that you can infuse with meaning, value, and purpose. It is simple: You do not need anything more than air to breathe, water to drink, and food to eat to keep you alive. Everything else is up to you to decide. It can be full of complications, or simple. The key is to examine your long-held beliefs, doctrines, and ideology passed on to you, often handed down from generation to generation, with no examination, questioning, or conscious consideration.

Many people explain life from a religious perspective based on the Bible. They preach to you that God created everything, and that everything God created is perfect. He never makes mistakes, so you should think that whatever happens is God's will, and that everything is going to be made right, eventually. There are certain rules to follow, and rule-breakers and non-believers will go to

Hell or face other persecution. What's interesting to me is that there are many interpretations of what is written in the Bible. But the good news is that you have the free will to choose what to believe.

There are, of course, other theories and explanations, and other answers to ultimate questions. From our point of view, Earth is huge, but when compared to the universe and all that exists, we suddenly look and feel so small, even microscopic. The discoveries that mankind has made in space are amazing, but our knowledge has limits, so the more we discover, the less we understand. Time and space have no limits: no beginning and no end. This is a concept that is difficult for the human mind to grasp.

Mankind has tried to explain why we are here, since the beginning. Why do we exist? Does life have a purpose? Most people believe that God created everything, and the rest of the people believe we are here by accident. Let me make you think for a minute. What if God does not even know you exist? What if the creation of mankind was more or less an accident?

Let me give you an example: I have planted wonderful fruit trees in my yard. Last year, I hung a birdfeeder from a limb in my big mango tree, and filled it up with seeds for the birds and squirrels to eat. A couple of weeks later, I came back to refill the little house with seeds of a different kind. To my surprise, there were several little seedlings that had sprouted right under that mango tree. Where a seed had fallen to the ground from the birdfeeder, and had taken root in the fertile soil, a tiny new plant emerged. It had not been my intent to plant these seeds and have them grow, yet here they were. Seeing an unexpected new little bright green plant struck me in the moment as somewhat profound.

What if the Earth is the plant that sprouted from a tiny seed that was once intended for a different purpose? What if God has yet to even notice our existence? Or, what if the God you imagine is not at all who or what God really is? I ask these questions, not because I want to change what you believe, but because I want you to understand that what you think and believe is the *logical answer*, might not be *the answer*, but only one of many possibilities.

Your beliefs may one day prove to be correct, but today, when we look at and analyze everything that exists in the universe, and how we are but a small grain of sand by comparison, you will recognize that maybe what you *know,* is not at all how things actually occur. I want you to keep one thing in mind. It doesn't matter what you choose to believe, as long as you live life by this principle: "Do unto others as you would have them do unto you."

These words are simple and uncomplicated. There is no need to cling to any ideology that complicates your life. Be wise and enjoy life itself. If you believe in God, can you imagine that part of God is inside of you? I believe that this part of Him is the giant who resides in you.

We Do Not Live Forever

Do you know how many people die every day, worldwide? According to the World Health Organization, 56 million people die every year. That's around 153,424 people who die every day. While we cannot constantly dwell on it, this reality should remind us that tomorrow is not promised, and that life must be cherished.

In the United States, statistics show that the average age of death is 79.5 years. This is an average, but the reason I like to mention it is because I notice that many people today act like they will live forever. If, on average, we live about 80 years, then how many days have you lived on this planet, and how many days do you have left? Today, as I'm reviewing this book to send it to be edited, I have lived 14,731 days. Consider that 80 years consists of around 29,220 days. How many have you lived, and how many do you have left? What if you earned a dollar for each day you lived. Would $29,220 be enough? The truth is, you may not be able to add more days to your life, but you can absolutely make sure that each day you live is well-spent.

Now, in order to live life wisely, you don't have to spend all your money. Many people today use the "life is short" excuse to buy huge houses and expensive cars, only to end up living their lives drowning in debt. This is what your monster tells you to do, but do you really want to spend half your life or more working like a slave in order to pay off those material items? I recently saw an offer for new car financing for seven years. At what point during your 2,556 days of car payments will that new car smell stop exciting you?

I hope you are getting the point that you cannot give your life in exchange for material things, and expect to be happy, because these things will not give you real happiness. You have to know how to enjoy life itself—without all of the possessions. (There's a reason they are called *trappings*.) Your monster LOVES trappings, and works overtime to provide creative justifications for you to fall into one trap after another. There is nothing on earth as short-sighted, determined, and mistaken as your monster in a greedy mood.

Your giant knows that nothing outside can satisfy the inside. When your inner self learns how to enjoy the non-material aspects of life, it becomes a fountain of happiness. This fountain nurtures the tree of life, such that it produces an abundance of excellent fruit. In other words, it produces excellent things externally.

Every second, minute, or hour that you live, will not be yours to live again. Unfortunately, we are unconscious about how we spend our time. If you were videotaped all day long, and then a report was generated, showing exactly how each hour was spent—how many minutes you were reading email, scrolling on social media, recounting your favorite complaints to others, watching television—you would be shocked. Not sure you agree? Take this challenge: Create a form on paper, a computer, or a smartphone, where you can make notes. Set a recurring alarm, and at the end of every single waking hour, write down how you spent that prior hour. For even better information, do it every half hour. This is just for your awareness; no one will see it, so don't fudge anything to *look good*. Keep these notes for seven days.

I don't know exactly what you will discover, but I promise it will be eye-opening and useful to you. One major benefit is that you will learn where your time expenditures are not congruent with your life mission. For example, if you are a business owner, and your time is being wasted on administrative details that could be delegated to others, it would make sense to instead work on things to help your company grow, by doing things that only you can do. You say you want your business to be successful, yet you are robbing it of your best efforts.

Your Giant or Your Monster

Also, by tracking yourself for seven days, you will discover your bad habits, and by doing so, you can begin to replace them with good habits. Only one habit can be dominant. Remember, we are creatures of habit, which means that the sum result of the day equals the sum of each habit we practiced, good or bad.

I mention all of this because we must take into account that we cannot leave everything for tomorrow or a future day. Time goes by very quickly, as if life is on a countdown. It is imperative that we develop good habits and stop wasting our precious time on unimportant nonsense. Remember, if I take your money, you can get more. If I take your house, you can buy another. But if I take away just one minute of your time, you can never get it back. When your giant is in control of your life, he will not allow you to waste your most precious resource: your time.

Actions to take now:

What **purpose** motivates you to push yourself to reach your maximum potential? What is your **life mission**? How many days have you lived on this planet?

Go to **www.buildingyourgiant.com/bonuses** to get access to the additional content on the website, watch bonus videos, about purpose and life mission. Also, on the website, you will find our Days Lived Calculator, to find out exactly how many days you have lived.

Your Giant or Your Monster

Notes

Chapter 4

Creating the Future You Desire

"Setting goals is the first step in turning the invisible into the visible."
– Tony Robbins

What Is a Goal?

A goal is an idea of **the future you desire**. It can be the intended result that a person or a group of people envisions, plans, and commits to achieve. People endeavor to reach goals within a finite time, by setting deadlines. If there is no "by when," it is not really a goal. Saying "I would like to see Alaska someday" is quite different than "I am planning to see Alaska before I turn 40 next year." It is easy to see which one is actually a goal—and importantly, which one is more likely to lead to creating the desired outcome.

For the first time in my life, in the year 2000, I heard that I needed to have **written goals**. I was listening to a program by Tony Robbins, where he explained the importance of having goals and writing down your progress in different areas of life, on a daily basis. That made sense to me, but the reality is that I did none of what he suggested. I did not find a notebook, I did not write down my goals, and I did not make a habit of assessing my goal-reaching progress on a daily basis. My goals remained in my mind, which I thought was good enough. The only thing I did at that time was to develop a financial plan. I organized a little in this area, but nothing more. After I got married, in 2003, my wife and I improved that financial plan, and enlarged it and made it more specific. But regarding the advice to always write down all of your goals, I continued as most people do, and kept them in my mind.

Years passed, and I continued listening not only to Tony Robbins, who always communicated the importance of writing goals down on paper, but to other motivational speakers who would say the same thing. (I was not actually listening, just hearing…) Each expert said how vital it was to the personal development of some successful person of which they spoke. Finally, I had heard the same thing so many times that I decided to really listen and to do it. (It is my deepest wish that you will use this opportunity, this book, to finally listen and take action. Rather than *someday*, why not now?)

For the past nine years, I've been writing my goals in a notebook. (I'm writing this book in 2019.) I have a different notebook for every year, and I also keep a notebook dedicated to my long-term goals and visions. What I want is for you to accomplish your goals a lot faster than the time it took me. If you apply what you are going to learn in this book, you will reach your success much sooner than you can even imagine. Do not wait another day to start. The longer you wait, the longer it will take you to achieve the success you desire.

Write down everything you want, even if it seems impossible to achieve, or silly, or weird. If you're hesitant because you don't know where to start, just begin writing, and little by little, you will begin to find clarity and specificity. By the time you finish reading this chapter, you will know how you are going to begin. Before you continue to the next, I want you to write your goals in different areas of your life. You must do this if you want to achieve great and wonderful things in your future. **If you don't do something completely different from what you have done in the past, the results of the future will not be different.**

I am the kind of person who believes that success is a path that we all must travel, and it takes less than one dollar to take the first step. Yes, with less than one dollar, you simply need to buy a notebook and a pencil. Do not use a pen to write down your goals. In life, nothing is set in stone; you will have to be flexible and adapt, and that's why I suggest a pencil. It is all part of the process. If you are wondering if you can use a laptop or tablet or other tool to make your goals list, then yes, you can do that, if that is what works best for you—but you must develop the habit of SEEING the goals every day, and updating your progress. For me, using notebooks makes it hard to forget.

Only 1% of the successful people I have met recommend that I should NOT have written goals, but rather that I should keep my goals clear in my mind. The other 99% have recommended I either write down my goals or that I **implement a system,** which, in my opinion, is the same thing because it requires **writing down** some kind of plan. So, if the majority of highly successful people recommend writing down your goals, why don't most people seeking success choose to do it? I'll tell you why.

What Do People Think of the Goals?

According to some expert opinions, only 3% of the population have written goals. To me, this explains why so many people in the world are unhappy and dissatisfied with their life's journey. Humans need goals to grow, and if we do not grow or advance, we become frustrated, and we begin to focus on all the negative things that surround us.

Whenever I meet someone who is struggling financially, I ask them: Do you have written goals? The answer is always the same: NO. If they tell me they want to own their own house, I ask: What kind of house would you like to have, and what price do you want to pay? In what time do you want to achieve those things? For all these questions, the answer is always the same: I DON'T KNOW. This is where the problem lies, because if your mind does not have these answers, it does not know how to look for ways to make your goals a reality.

Most people **do not know exactly what they want in life,** and that is why they do not achieve much. If they do achieve something, they usually accomplished it the hard way. Others think that if they set goals and do not reach them quickly enough, they will only get frustrated, upset, or depressed. They also tell you that if they set goals, they feel pressure to reach them, which creates constant stress. Let's be realistic: The things you really want in life, that are of any value, will require you to make an effort to acquire them. Many times, life will not go as planned, and you will feel frustrated and sometimes stressed. But remember, the person who does not give up is the one who triumphs and ends up in a position to better help others.

Now, let me share with you the reason I didn't write my goals from the first moment it was suggested to me, so that you do not fall into the same trap. Remember how we've been talking about your giant and your monster? When it comes to writing down your goals, what do you think the monster wants you to do? Of course, **your monster does not want you to have them. Why?** Well, the **first reason** is that you have never done this before, and change like this scares your monster. **The second reason** is that when you write what you want to achieve, you will have to take action to achieve it, but the lazy monster would rather do nothing. The **third reason** is that when you write your goals, you will realize that you have to leave your comfort zone, and your monster absolutely hates this fact the most.

If you decide to wait for years, like I did, without writing your goals down, despite the evidence to do otherwise, **your monster is in control of your life**. Your monster is an unbeliever, and anyone who has spent life listening to other people who are also controlled by their monster, has the wrong mentality. The monster does not let you see the potentially wonderful things ahead in your future. He tells you that the next 10 years of your life will be the same as the past 10 years, and he is going to prove it to you by discouraging you from living life any differently than you have been. But I wrote this book for people who want to make changes, who want their giant to be in control, and I want you to be one of them. Take the first step to becoming a part of the small percentage of people that decides to be extraordinary. Change your life and those of others.

What Is the Difference Between a Goal and a Purpose?

I will start by telling you that *goal* and *purpose* are inseparable, because if you have goals, you must have a purpose in mind, and if you have a purpose, you need to have the goals to achieve it. In order words, *you have to set up goals that are in alignment with your purpose. The more you stay focused on your purpose, the easier it is to achieve your goals.* Imagine that you have just established your own company, and you want to make a million dollars in sales within two years, or maybe you want to employ 100 people, or reach half a million customers that will benefit from your services; those are your long-term goals. Write down your long-term goals and put them in a place where you can see them every day. Now, you must develop a plan, or a step-by-step system to accomplish those goals. Write down what you have to do, every day, week, month, quarter or every year (these are your short-term goals), in order to achieve your long-term goals. If you have short-term and long-term goals, you will have more confidence on your way to reach the summit of your purpose.

Let me give you an example: Imagine that you have to reach the top of a mountain at night, but to accomplish this feat, you must walk through a narrow and dangerous path, in the dark. Fortunately, you have a flashlight in your hand, and when you turn it on, you can see where you are going to walk. Undoubtedly, with a flashlight, you could walk with less trepidation and more confidence, reaching the mountain's peak much quicker. The goals are like this flashlight on your way to success; they are essential because they show you where you are going, and help you get there faster. Consider now that with the flashlight, you can only see what is directly in front of you; you cannot see the entire path you must take to reach the top of the mountain. **When**

you have a great and important purpose, quite often you are unsure of how you are going to achieve it. This is normal. You may not be able to envision the entire path to your success, but by setting reachable goals, little by little, you will discover ways to make it happen.

Remember that I mentioned previously how much I hated school when I was younger; I particularly disliked reading. One day I realized, however, that to achieve the things I wanted in life, I had to read—especially personal development books. I wanted to read a lot of them, but I just really hated reading. My purpose, was to develop a habit of reading every day to improve myself. What did I do first? I bought the book, *Think Like a Winner,* by Dr. Walter Doyle Staples, and I decided to read one page every day. This was my goal, **no matter how tired I was, and no matter what else was going on in my life.** I set out on my goal and, while I struggled to overcome my disdain of reading at first, within a very short period of time, I learned to love it. The moment I finished this one book, I was eager to start the next. I could literally feel my mind growing as I kept feeding it knowledge. By the way I highly recommend this book.

By now, I hope you have noticed something very important: It's the little things that count—the little and consistent things. If I had forced myself to read for one or two hours every day, for a week or more, I probably would have ended up hating reading even more. Because I started slowly and gave myself a small but realistic goal to just read every day—for no specified amount of time—I made progress little by little, until a habit developed. Today, I just want to be reading all the time. The same principles apply to anything else you want to accomplish. When I set out to accomplish this, I made a commitment to myself and my giant.

Once your giant is involved, the last thing you want is to break your commitment and let your giant down. This is a key to achieving what you want, but many people don't understand this concept, because they are controlled by their monster. It's the reason they don't accomplish their purposes in their lives, much less the goals to achieve them.

I'll give you another example: Every January, there are people everywhere we look, resolving to get healthy. They join gyms, buy expensive workout clothes, and start exercising every day for an hour or so. Come February, they lose their motivation and continue to pay a gym membership for a gym they no longer show up to. But if your definite **purpose** truly is to get healthy, lose weight, look better, or all of the above, you must set the goals to get you there. Remember, start small. You could commit to spending 10 minutes every day walking around your neighborhood. Then, either add time to your walk or choose to run 10 minutes instead. Next, start to eat an apple a day, or add one extra serving of vegetables to your meal. Swapping out your old habits for better ones can be both rewarding and fun. The idea is to make simple changes, little by little. When you do it in this manner, the goal helps you to develop the **habit of consistency**, which in turn becomes a positive lifestyle change, getting you one step closer to achieving your purpose. So, whether you want to buy a house or a car, or have your own business, think about the purpose or the reasons. Remember what you do on a daily basis to accomplish this purpose, are your short-term goals.

The Magic of Writing What You Want

When I look at my past, one thing that I regret is that I didn't write down my goals sooner, because, as I know now, there is magic in doing so. Listen, if you want to achieve the most important things in life faster, I believe you should put them in writing. You have to be specific, and you have to set goals in different areas of your life. This is **essential** to achieve what you want. After you write your goals, look at your notepad every day, if possible. When you start doing this, you will be surprised, because all these things that you write and analyze every day will be recorded, not only in your conscious mind but also in your subconscious mind.

The first magical thing that will happen, when you write what you want, is that these things become a **magnet** that will gradually pull you to where you want to go. But how can they pull you if you do not even have them written? How can they pull you if they are not a clearly defined part of your life? This is one of the most powerful tools that you can use right now. This is not for everybody; it is only for those people who want **more**. **More** is one of the most common words used by humans to describe how much of something we want. We want *more* air, *more* money, *more* water, *more* food, *more* happiness, *more* peace, *more* love, etc. Even at the end of our lives, we often wish we had *more* time. There is nothing wrong with always wanting more, as long as you do not lose your balance or become greedy.

The second magical thing that occurs, when you write down your wants, is that you begin to see more clearly what it is that you really desire. *Clarity is power, so you must visualize your goals and your purposes as if you've already accomplished them.* Focus your energy on these accomplishments, and it will be easier for your giant to get you there.

I'm not here to tell you what your goals should be in your life, but I want to remind you that human beings are motivated by goals and objectives. When I see a person that has no motivation, I know it is because they have no goals, no objectives, or purposes, and nothing to light their soul on fire and keep it burning. They do not understand the value of improvement and growth. Often, they exist through life, feeling unhappy and depressed. The person who has goals and purposes in their life has a fire that not only heats their soul but also warms everyone who approaches them.

In my notebooks, I like to write what I want to achieve every year, in different areas of my life. I always write things that are realistic, even if at the time they feel impossible to achieve. Then, I take action, and I start working to reach my goals, and I accomplish what I once thought was impossible. Have a clear, written plan of what you want in your life, so that you can visualize it step by step. Little by little, you can make your dreams a reality.

The Power of Visualization

Imagine the following scenario: Today we sign a contract in which I guarantee that in three years I will pay you $3 million. No matter where you live in the world, this is a lot of money! There are terms to this contract, though, and you have to meet all the requirements stated within it. The requirements are as follows:

1. Write all your goals in a notebook, and work hard to achieve them.
2. Work to achieve and maintain good physical health for the

three years, by exercising at least one hour, three times a week, and eating healthy.
3. Read every day about business and personal development so that you have the correct mentality.
4. Over the three years, you cannot waste time on unimportant things, and you have to dedicate quality time to your family on a daily basis.
5. Improve in a significant way as a person and in every area of your life.
6. Learn to speak in public, in an effective way.

That's all! Nothing that I asked of you is impossible to achieve, even though the truth is that it may not always be easy. Anyone can follow these steps and fulfill these requirements, but can you guess why most people don't? Because they do not have a guaranteed payday of $3 million coming their way after three years, and they simply do not believe that they will be able to achieve such amazing results on their own. Your giant knows that if you set your mind to do these things, your future will be wonderful, not only because of what you will achieve, but because of the person you will become. But you need to **visualize what you want and see yourself already achieving it.** If you make a commitment to work on these tasks every day, your giant knows that your success is guaranteed, as if it were a signed contract.

When you fulfill one of your goals, even if what you have achieved is something small, you will feel the motivation to strive to reach another. With each accomplishment, your mind produces endorphins that will make you feel happier and give you more energy and motivation. Remember, the first step is to write the goals. If you manage to do this, you have achieved something great, but it is very important that **you make the decision and commit yourself,** so that you achieve what you propose. Then, remember to visualize the things you want as *already done,* so that you find the necessary motivation to succeed.

In my life, my giant was able to see myself owning the home of my dreams and having it paid off. My giant was able to see me with the woman of my dreams. My giant was able to see me financially free. Today, my giant can see me getting all my family out of poverty. My giant can see me becoming so wealthy that I have to devote a lot of time to planning where all my gifts and charitable contributions will go.

Your giant must have a good vision of your future, because your monster can't even see the good things that will happen to you tomorrow. He is pessimistic and negative; he's always trying to protect you from what could go wrong. If you see life through the eyes of your monster, you will live a life of darkness and regrets.

The Law of Attraction

The third magical thing that happens, when you have your written goals, is that you start using the **Law of Attraction.** Remember that what you focus on expands. People who have achieved great success call this law **the secret**, because many people do not even know that it exists. Even worse, in my opinion, is that most people, when the secret is revealed to them, still do not believe in or use it. This is one of the reasons why not everyone in life gets everything they want. You must learn more about this law, and know how it works, because it is not as easy as sitting on your couch asking for material possessions and riches to suddenly appear. As we've discussed, you have to set goals and work to fulfill them, but what often happens is that after setting your goals, you don't have the slightest idea how to achieve them. This is where the law of attraction can lead you to the ideas, people, and opportunities that you need. Now, make sure that you keep one thing in mind: **It's the action behind the law of attraction that will transform your dreams into reality.**

Our perception is our reality. The law of attraction is not the only law available to you, but it is one of the most powerful. This law creates our reality and is always working in our favor or against what we want, based on our perceptions and thoughts. I can also say that we attract more of what we already are.

To be more specific, I have noticed that when a person starts to think, for example, that he is going to have an accident, and dwells on this happening, sooner or later it does. If you go through life thinking that you will be robbed at home, or that your car will be stolen, sooner or later, this will also happen. If you constantly worry that you are going to get sick or contract a disease, eventually you will. That's how the law of attraction works against you, and most people don't even know it. If you are always thinking that bad things always happen to you, and that nothing ever goes your way, that is exactly how your life will continue. You must understand that everything starts inside you, in your way of thinking. If this law can work against you, it has to work the other way around too, don't you think?

Consider this: You can spend precious time and energy swimming in the mud, persistent and determined, but it does not mean that you are going to get anywhere. To get a different result, you have to do something different. If you have never used the law of attraction in your favor, start now. Be consistent, and you will be surprised what happens. **When the negative thoughts begin to come to your mind, reject them immediately. They are the work of your inner monster.** When negative thoughts and ideas pass through your mind, replace them instead with something positive, such as your purpose and your goals. Just as quickly as changing the channel on your TV, flip your thoughts to those that are empowering. *Remain focused on all the wonderful things you have in your life now, and that you will have in the future.*

The inner struggle that we all face will be with us for life, without exception. **If you think that more bad things happen to you than to others, I guarantee you that will be the case, and those bad things will continue to happen.** But if you begin thinking and believing that you are one of the most fortunate people, more and better things will come your way. I hope you understand the point I'm trying to make. If you don't, read this paragraph again. *This law can either help you or hurt you; the amazing thing is that you are the person who decides.*

We create our own realities—our own circumstances—through our thoughts. I understand that it may not be easy at first to get carried away by these positive thoughts. That is because we have become accustomed to our monster telling us that it is unrealistic to expect only good things to happen to us. Now is the time to stop listening to your monster, and start listening to your giant, who knows the limitless possibilities of your fortune and blessings. And when any successful person tells you to do something, listen to them too, and put into practice what you hear. This is priceless wisdom that can help you achieve the same amazing successes, simply by making an effort to work more effectively on yourself.

Are You Satisfied with Your Achievements?

Over the years, I have had the privilege of meeting some very rich and successful people. I always ask myself: If this person were to lose everything he or she has, how long would it take for him or her to recover everything back, and more? The answer is always the same: one or two years. Why? It is because of the person they have become, because of their good habits, discipline, knowledge, attitude, and self-confidence. Mainly, it is because each of these ultra-successful people is someone who lives with purpose, and I know that success will follow them wherever they apply themselves.

> *"You can have more than you have because you can become more than you are."*
> – Jim Rohn

No matter where you are, you can always become more, if you have a purpose. Nothing can stop you, but you have to work on your inner giant in order to reach that higher level.

Most people don't live like they have a purpose—don't be like most people. While it does not have to be this way, the sad truth is that most people in this world are controlled by their monster. Your monster wants to keep you poor and weak in every way. But, you can decide to be different, to not be like most people, in order to discover your full potential.

There are many people who have inspired me in my life, but the man who has filled me with admiration, inspiration, and humility is Nicholas James Vujicic. Nick Vujicic was born in Australia and, at the age of 36, is married with four children. He has written many books, acted in movies and television shows, and has dedicated his life to being a global inspiration by praising and encouraging people to be the best they can be. For me, he has been a great source of inspiration, and he is a source of inspiration for all the people who know him. So, what is so special about Nick? Well, he was born with no arms and no legs, but with a huge heart.

Consider how many people—able-bodied with no disabilities—do nothing of importance with their lives. What makes Nick Vujicic different? In my opinion, it is simply that he is led by his inner giant. He has admitted that, understandably, he's been through some very tough times, but he overcame them and persevered. Nick is proof that the greatest disability that exists in the world today is non-physical: It is mental. We are all capable of amazing things; we just have to decide to be different and to build up our inner giant. We all have a giant within, but it is up to each person to acknowledge and appreciate him, and to let him take control.

> "This is the true joy in life, the being used for a purpose recognized by yourself as a mighty one; the being thoroughly worn out before you are thrown on the scrap heap; the being a force of Nature instead of a feverish selfish little clod of ailments and grievances complaining that the world will not devote itself to making you happy."
> – George Bernard Shaw

Actions to take now:

To help your giant you need to have long-term and short-term goals! Start writing everything you truly want to achieve in life. Start with the small, and then write the big things. Next, write what you will do each day, each week, each month, each quarter, or throughout the year to help you accomplish these goals and purposes. Be specific but realistic as you write down what you desire to achieve in the following areas of your life: spiritually, mentally, emotionally; and physical health, , relationships, economic status, material possessions, and what you want to do for others. Complete this step before continuing to the next chapter, but then read on, because you still have a lot to learn about your giant.

Notes

Chapter 5

What Is My Secret Formula?

"Without a formula, there is no paradise."
— Josue Lopez

The Magic Pills

Wouldn't you like to be able to take a pill that would offer you all the results you wanted overnight? Imagine a pill for HEALTH that keeps you healthy for the rest of your life, allowing you to eat whatever you want without gaining weight. You would no longer have to do any kind of exercise, and you would be full of energy. You would never get sick, and at the end of your life, at a ripe old age, you'd be guaranteed a peaceful death, without any pain and suffering. Wow! Wouldn't that be wonderful? All of the health issues that worry most of humanity would cease to exist.

How about a second pill, the pill of HAPPINESS? Simply take it before going to bed, and when you wake up, you will have happiness, peace, and love for the rest of your life. Never again will you feel sad, anxious, or depressed. All of your negative feelings would be a thing of the past. Take a few minutes and think of an occasion in your life when you felt like that, full of happiness, peace, and love. Maybe when you fell in love for the first time, or when you were on your honeymoon. Perhaps you felt that way when you managed to win an important game or achieve a great goal. Feeling this way for the rest of your life would be fantastic!

Now, envision a third pill, the MONEY pill. This pill would grant you the ability to know exactly how to manage your money. You would know what kind of business you should start, and how to make it grow so that, in a year, it produces millions of dollars in revenue. You would know how to invest your money so that it produces more money, for the rest of your life. Money would come to you in abundance and, with it, you would be able to purchase all the material possessions your heart desires: cars, houses, boats, and even airplanes and helicopters. At the end of your life, you would leave behind enough money to ensure your family's financial security and comfort, while also being able to donate a large sum of money to your favorite cause. Your family, friends, and millions of people around the world would remember you as a person who strived to do good for humanity.

How great would it be if it was as easy as that? Obviously, these magic pills don't exist, but it is still possible to achieve the health, happiness, and money you yearn for. In fact, the last thing we really want are magic pills that would rob us of dreaming, achieving, and enjoying our accomplishments with satisfaction. There is a simple formula that, if learned and used properly, will lead you to achieve everything you want in your life. The proof is in the millions of achievements, some on a large scale and others on a smaller scale, which people all over the world, including me, have accomplished.

What Is My Secret Formula?

The DKAR Formula

The name of this formula is **D+K+A=R**. To help you remember, it's pronounced like *"the car."* This formula will be your car or vehicle, or the means by which you will travel on your journey to building your inner giant, overcoming obstacles, and improving your life in every capacity. No matter what level you are at in your life, be it good or bad, you must always continue to grow. As humans, if **we are not growing, we are dying.** The more we grow, the more we can *level up* and put ourselves in a better position to help others.

Now, let me explain this formula. Each letter represents an important word:

DISCIPLINE
+
KNOWLEDGE
+
ACTION
=
RESULTS

You need to be **disciplined** to acquire **knowledge,** then you need to take **action,** and if you have all three, you will get the **results** you want.

These words seem very simple; but in them, you will find the secret to achieve what you want. I use this formula every day to improve and grow in all aspects of my life. I invite you to meditate on it to see if you like it too. Each person has their own philosophy, their own way of seeing things, their own system to learn, and you must look for a system that works for you. The most important thing is that whatever you choose to live by, it should give you results. If you are not getting the results you want, try this formula.

Everything you see in your life is the result of what you do NOT see. In other words, the invisible creates the visible. Think of a speaker talking from a stage. You notice that this person is a very competent speaker. The way they articulate their words draws you in, telling stories that leave you amazed and eager to listen. In this example, the speaker themselves, with their confidence and conviction, is what you are able to see. However, what you did not see is all the time that they invested, practicing and memorizing, to be able to stand up in front of an audience and keep them captivated with their words. Just like the speaker, to get results, you have to have a process that works for you: a formula to get you to your goal. With the D.K.A.R formula, and doing one thing at a time, you can accomplish just that.

Discipline

In the D.K.A.R formula, DISCIPLINE is the first component. Personal discipline is an essential key for every human being. The immense lack of personal discipline has led mankind to many of the great challenges it faces today, and that's because so many people are being controlled by their monster. Your monster doesn't know what personal discipline is, but your giant is an expert in it. Discipline leads you to, and guides you through, the steps you need to follow in order to grow. Your giant thrives when you are disciplined.

What Is My Secret Formula?

I'll give you an example: I like coconuts, especially when they are cold, and even better if you add a splash of coconut rum to the juice. I also like the white mass inside of them, even more so when sprinkled with sugar. Think of a coconut palm tree. What do you think causes it to produce coconuts full of sweet water and white meat inside? Hint: it's the part you *don't see*. It's all in the roots. If the roots of the coconut palm are unhealthy, the coconut may be small, without meat, or with very little water, or even worse, the tree may not produce any coconuts at all.

Take stock of your fruits. Are they filled with fleshy meat, and filled with clean, tasty water? Or are they dry, black, and empty inside? To know the answer, look at your life, and look around you. Are you **pleased** with everything you have? Notice that I didn't say grateful, as we should all be grateful—just being alive is wonderful, and we can always feel grateful for everything good that surrounds us. But being pleased is another thing. If you are happy with the person you are, and with what you have achieved in every way, then your coconuts or your fruits have been nourished by very healthy roots (or habits). Now, if you don't like the fruits you see, then you have big problems in your roots; **that is, in your way of thinking and acting (your habits).** It is nobody else's fault that you are not pleased with your fruit, because each one of us is responsible for our own actions and lives, which means that we also have the power to heal our damaged roots, with personal DISCIPLINE.

There is a saying: "**Everything you want is on the other side of your fears.**" I don't argue with this, but I would add that "**everything you want can be achieved with personal discipline.**" Yokoi Kenji says: *"Discipline will exceed intelligence."* These are wise words. I used to think that to be successful you needed to be very intelligent, but I learned that this is not necessarily true. You just have to be disciplined. If you doubt that your giant is as capable as the giants of other successful people, that is only because it is what your monster wants you to think. When the monster's voice comes on, change the channel! Listen to your giant. Have the **discipline to acquire the knowledge** you need, and you will be surprised by what your giant is capable of doing.

Let me ask you a question: How do you know if you are a disciplined person? The answer is very simple: If you can control yourself at all times. In other words, if **you have mastery over yourself to only do things of value.** It's that simple, but for many, it seems impossible.

Imagine having control over all your actions, emotions, and feelings, etc., all the time. Can you imagine what kind of person you could become? I want you to know that this is possible. **If you set out to do it right now, little by little, you can create the habits of listening and obeying your inner giant, not your monster.** You have to commit yourself right now, and keep this commitment for the rest of your life. If you do, I guarantee that you will be extraordinary. If you are thinking that all of this makes sense but it is not easy, I will tell you that this is true for your monster. Your inner giant, however, has the power, the conviction, and the strength needed to achieve it. Step by step, you can lead your giant down the right path, until having control over your actions, emotions, and feelings becomes second nature.

What Is My Secret Formula?

Knowledge

To elevate yourself to the next level in your life, and achieve everything you dream, it is imperative that you acquire knowledge, and there is no better way to learn than through reading. The formula is simple: You need DISCIPLINE TO GAIN KNOWLEDGE. It is essential that you make a habit of reading. Ask the people in your life, who seem to be struggling, whether they habitually read every day. Chances are that their answer will be something along the lines of, "I don't like to read." Maybe there are others in your life who do read regularly, yet their lives are chaotic and disastrous. Why do you think that is? I will tell you. It's because they are **only** reading things like bad news, science fiction, novels, or other periodicals that don't produce any real benefit in their lives. These are your inner monster's favorite reading materials.

Have the discipline to read on a daily basis, but read what successful people read, such as books on **PERSONAL DEVELOPMENT**. Read about concepts and ideas that, once you learn them, will have an impact on your life and help you to improve. Books that teach you how to have a positive attitude, recognize opportunities, stay motivated every day to overcome any challenges that come your way, and that nourish and strengthen your inner giant so that it becomes invincible, are the kind of materials that will put you on the right path for you to change your life. **Acquiring specific knowledge will help you to achieve your goals.** Let me give you an example.

When I first entered the business of buying houses to flip and rent, I did so without any prior knowledge. I read no books, and didn't think to find an experienced mentor to guide me; and for this reason, I fell into several traps. When buying a house in the United States, with cash, it can be especially risky. Shortly after purchasing one without any financial assistance from the bank, I learned that it had been sold to me without a *clean title*. . According to the bank that I bought the house from, they "didn't know that there was another mortgage on the home." Because I had signed the paperwork without the proper knowledge to know exactly what I was signing, I could not sue the bank, or the title company. I had no leg to stand on.

My friend, Samuel, and I had invested in the home together. At first, it was an exciting challenge to restore an outdated home and then either rent it out as an income property or sell it for a profit. It took us two and a half months to fix, doing most of the work ourselves, and we already had an interested buyer lined up. Sounds perfect, right? One afternoon, I arrived home after a long day of fixing up the house. In front of my house, a small car was parked, and from it, an old lady emerged. She handed me a package, and she told me to sign a paper. Still not aware that the title on the recently purchased house was *dirty*, I asked her what all those papers were for. She informed me that someone was suing me for $150,000 dollars for the property I had bought. According to the person suing me, he had loaned money to the previous owners, and the owners hadn't paid him back.

Even though it took almost two and a half years of dealing with lawyers to get the situation resolved, Samuel and I were fortunate because we didn't lose much of our money. Compared to the $150,000 we were being sued for, the $8,000 I spent to hire a lawyer for legal advice was minimal. Nonetheless, it was $8,000 I could have potentially saved if I had been more knowledgeable about the business before going into it. Another lesson I learned

What Is My Secret Formula?

throughout this process is that justice is **green.** If you don't have the money to hire a lawyer to defend you and walk you through the various proceedings, you will lose. Even the lawyer assigned to me by the title insurance company of the property wanted me to accept the loss and close the case. They were not on my side, but the lawyer I was able to hire with my own money was. Of course, if I had to do it again, I'd have invested beforehand the $1,000 or so it takes to hire a competent lawyer who could review the paperwork and ensure I was making an informed purchase. This is knowledge I gained the hard way. This is a very long story, but the good news is that we didn't lose the property.

This is why I encourage you to acquire knowledge by doing simple things like reading a book or finding a mentor, especially before getting into any business. It will help you avoid many headaches and wasted time and money in your life. But if you don't first have the discipline to acquire knowledge, many great unnecessary challenges await you on the road to success. Always remember, **having knowledge gives you control over your life.** Develop a habit of learning something new every day, and your life will change for the better.

Now you need the DISCIPLINE to take ACTION. I have known people in my life who know so much that they are like human encyclopedias; but it doesn't serve them to know it all, because they never take **action.** It's like knowing all the perfect methods for paddling a small boat in open water, but letting the wind and current control where you travel, instead. Actions are what will take you where you want to go, and will ultimately give you the results you want.

Taking Action Gets Your Mind in the Mood

Do not make the mistake of waiting until you feel ready to take a particular action. Most people wait for their mood to motivate them to action, which does not work. Rather, taking actions will lead to your mood being elevated.

After writing your goals, step by step, then you have to take action—take the first step. For example, my purpose is to be able to help many to live better lives, and to motivate and teach people to rise to the next level in their lives. What goals have I set? I had to learn to speak in public, so I committed to speak in front of a group of people, a minimum of once a week. By the way, I strongly advise you to find a place where you could learn this, too.

Personally, I joined Toastmasters International, which is a club that operates worldwide, with many local chapters, for the purpose of promoting communication, leadership, and public speaking skills. Toastmasters brings members together to practice, learn, grow, mentor, and share, and when I found a chapter in my area, I took the action of showing up. I want you to know that just the idea of entering a room full of strangers terrified me. This was because of my inner monster that didn't want to do anything new. I made the decision that my monster does not control me, and I continued to take the actions to overcome my fear of public speaking, on my way to fulfilling my goals and purpose.

Don't get me wrong; I took action little by little. After all, being **consistent is not** about doing something today, and then two months from now, doing something else; rather, it **is about being**

What Is My Secret Formula?

disciplined, and perseverance is better than speed. After a year, I had improved greatly.

When I set the **goal** of writing a book, nobody believed me, much less my monster, because I didn't know how to type, and I had never written anything in Spanish or English. Only my own internal giant believed that I could do it. Once again, I put my goal in writing, and started little by little. Unfortunately, on day one, I began to doubt myself. I had no idea what went into writing a book and, to be honest, felt like it was never going to happen. But then I realized, that was my monster trying to take control.

My inner giant assured me that, while I didn't know what I was doing, I was going to learn—one sentence, one paragraph, one page at a time. After a year, the book was almost done. I still don't know how to write, and that's a good thing. Editors have to make a living, too! **Remember, the monster is always looking for evidence to prove to you that you can't achieve what you want.** He'll try to convince you that you are not intelligent enough, you are wasting your time, you will fail, everyone will laugh at you, and you should give up. On a daily basis, your monster will try to tell you these things, but your response to him should simply be: THANK YOU FOR SHARING YOUR OPINION. Then, go about your business of taking the actions necessary to accomplish your dreams and aspirations. Your monster only wants to protect your body and your ego, but with the giant on your side, you have all the protection you need.

To write my first book I used the D.K.A.R. formula and, after writing for a few months, noticed that I was improving. I was writing better content at a faster pace. I kept doing this until I managed to publish my first eBook on Amazon.com. It was less than 50 pages, but I achieved it! So, you see, I didn't know how, and it seemed impossible, but I used the discipline to acquire the knowledge I needed, and then had the discipline to take the actions, step by step, until I accomplished my goal. There is no other secret—it is that simple.

This is what makes people different: Some are willing to do what it takes, and others are not. If you make a commitment to implement the formula in all areas of your life, you will grow, guaranteed. As you reach your goals, you will become more confident, you will have more knowledge, you will believe in yourself more, and you will feel excited and motivated because you achieved something that seemed impossible. You'll realize that you can achieve anything you want, all because you decided to take action.

Results

If you already completed what was suggested in the previous chapters, then you know exactly, or have a clear idea of, what the results are that you seek in every aspect of your life. This is great because, in order for this formula to work, the first thing you have to pinpoint is the desired RESULT. I want you to ask yourself at this moment: What are the final results I want in life? Most people don't truly know what they want in life, and when they think they know, they usually respond with things like: money, a more beautiful home, love, and happiness. None of these answers are wrong, but they do little to guide us, because they are very general answers that don't have any clarity or focus. In order to bring positive change and improvement to your life, you must know **exactly** what that change or improvement looks like. What is the **specific result** you want to obtain in any area of your life?

To give you an example, nobody wants money. Money is a dirty, (and usually) crumpled up piece of paper. That's all it is! The value of money is not in the money itself but in what that money can give us. With that in mind, reconsider the result: Is it food and water, a clean and secure home, a reliable car, a nice boat, family vacations all over the world, a college fund for your children? Do you understand now that the specific result we wish to achieve goes far beyond just money?

One of the results that I personally wanted for my life was to have a big boat and to learn to fish in the deep sea, so I could go out with friends and family and catch large fish. I spent eight years raising money for a boat, during which time I did no fishing. Before buying the boat, however, I began spending time with my friend, Alejandro, who knew how to fish. From him, I not only learned how to fish but also learned about boats. Soon, the two of us decided to invest in a boat together—result achieved.

You can see that I did not achieve this result overnight. First, I had to decide exactly what the **result** was that I wanted. Second, I had to have the discipline to gather money and to acquire knowledge. There were moments that I got invited to go fishing after having worked all day and all the previous night. I was tired, but I went anyway. Learning to fish also required expenses—deep sea fishing is not cheap—but I did whatever it took. I was disciplined, I acquired the knowledge, and I took action. Yes, it took time, but in the end, I got the result I wanted. Today, I have my own boat, and when I want to go fishing in deep waters, it is only a matter of making the time to enjoy the fruits of my labor.

Perhaps the result you want is to find a spouse and start a family. Perfect! For this, my formula also works. **You just have to be disciplined to become the person you need to be so that you can attract the person you want to have by your side.** Hopefully, at this stage in your life, you know yourself, but because a relationship and marriage are a partnership, it's also important to *know the opposite sex.* (Notice I didn't say *understand* the opposite sex, since sometimes understanding is impossible!). To achieve this, you need the discipline to acquire knowledge through reading or learning from people who have been able to achieve a happy and lasting marriage. If you do this before looking for a spouse, you will avoid many headaches, because we are all very different. Many people don't do well with their spouse, and the main reason is because they don't know enough about the opposite sex.

Finally, you've got to take action, because if you don't take action, there is no movement—you understand. You can become the person you wish to be, study and know the opposite sex, use prayer, the law of attraction, or whatever other methods to attract a mate, but if you don't decide to take action by having the courage to go out there and meet other people, you will never succeed in finding the ideal spouse. And yes, I said *ideal* spouse, because finding a spouse is easy, but finding the right person for you requires D.K.A.R.

What Is My Secret Formula?

Actions to take now:

Promise yourself and your giant that from now on, you will apply this D.K.A.R. formula in every aspect of your life; but start small, and don't rush the process. Pick one thing that you will start doing today, and use the D.K.A.R. formula to achieve it. Remember, reading is an excellent way to acquire the knowledge you'll need to achieve your results. One book that you should read after this one: *The Compound Effect,* by Darren Hardy.

Your Giant or Your Monster

Notes

Chapter 6

What Tools Can You Use Right Now?

"Thoughts and beliefs are the seeds of success."
– Josue Lopez

The Power of the Mind

You need tools to be able to complete most jobs. If you work in an office, think about all the things you use, like computers, pens, pencils, printers, etc. If you work in construction, or as a mechanic, or you are a doctor, tools are necessary to help you perform your job with precision and efficiency. Even within our homes, we rely on various tools to perform tasks. Tools have always been, and will always be, a part of our lives.

But what about the tool that we all possess from birth? Our mind. **Most people do not know or believe that everything they need to create the life that they want to live is contained in their head.** Our mind is the most powerful tool; we just have to use it the right way to get the result we want.

In most cases where the monster is in control and not the giant, people demonstrate that their minds are full of unnecessary junk.

The first step in growing your giant requires eliminating the negative thinking, so that there is more room for positive thinking. If you do not have the habit of thinking correctly and positively, it is likely that nothing else will work in your favor. But if you can manage to keep your thoughts in order, it will be much easier to develop good ideas, and good ideas are more valuable than money.

As one of the 7.5 billion people on this planet, you must reach your maximum potential. You deserve the best, so you must not settle for misery. One of the biggest problems that humanity faces is having the wrong beliefs. Now is the time to analyze your beliefs. Do you think you are condemned to be poor? That belief is simply wrong. Like these beliefs, we have many in our heads, and that is why we do not reach excellence in everything. Do not stop reading this book. Put into practice everything that you will learn from it, and little by little, you will be surprised how your life will change for the better. You will be amazed by the material things you will obtain, but what will surprise you the most is the person you will become.

Your Thoughts

We become what we think. Many of the wisest people, in the past and present, agree with this statement. So, it would be wise for us to really think about these words and ask ourselves: What am I constantly thinking about? In the book, *Think like a Winner,* by Dr. Walter Doyle Staples, he writes something that I like to call the six magic words. This is his explanation:

> "When you change your way of thinking,
> you change your beliefs,

What Tools Can You Use Right Now?

> when you change your beliefs,
> you change your expectations,
> when you change your expectations,
> you change your attitude.
> When you change your attitude,
> you change your behavior.
> When you change your behavior,
> you change your performance.
> When you change your performance,
> you change your life. "

So, again, I encourage you to ask yourself: What am I constantly thinking about? Am I'm constantly thinking about what I'm going to eat? About how I can pay my debts? Am I thinking about all the bad things that can happen to me? Am I thinking in term of scarcity or abundance? Am I a negative and pessimistic person? Am I always thinking that I will never be financially free or rich? You have to pay attention to what is on your mind all the time. Is your giant doing your thinking or is your monster?

Remember that we become what we think. Some people, after reading this book, will feel like they have a brand-new brain, because they never let their giant use it. Thus far, they've been too busy to think, or too busy thinking about the wrong things. It really is no wonder that most people around the world don't live the life they want to live. They focus on all the negative aspects of their lives, on all the negative aspects of other people, on the negative aspects of their country, and on the negative aspects of the planet. They want to live a good life, but to them, it is impossible!

If you want to identify what your thoughts have been in your past, look at everything you have today. **If you want to know what you will have in the future, pay attention to what you are thinking at this moment.** Do you like your current thoughts? Remember something: Your giant has no limits, and you do not have to think small; you can think big and in a very positive way. That's why he is called the *giant*! Focus on all the good and wonderful things of the present, and the good that awaits you in the future.

Napoleon Hill, in his book, *Think and Grow Rich* (which is a must-read), recommends that we spend at least 30 minutes a day thinking about the person we want to be. Let me give you an example: I want to be a professional speaker and trainer. Every day, I spend time thinking about it, as well as about the person I have to become in order to persuade and influence people to take control of their lives and make positive changes. You should do the same. Think of the person you want to be today and in the future. Think about where you want to be physically, mentally, and spiritually, and in your level of happiness, in your family, economic position, etc. Do you want to own your own business? Perhaps you want to become a doctor or a lawyer, or maybe a pilot. No matter your dream, begin spending your time thinking about what your life will be like *when*, not *if*, you become the person you dream of being.

Most people do not take time to think, but if you want to live a better life, you can't be like most people. You'll have to do something different to get a different result. You have to spend time, every day, thinking about how you will improve things for yourself, for your family, and for other people. When your giant gets into the habit of thinking correctly, this will be the first step

What Tools Can You Use Right Now?

on the right path to achieving everything you want.

Your Belief System (BS)

When you analyze your own beliefs, you will realize that most of what you believe is not your own organic beliefs; rather, they are the beliefs of other people that have been transmitted to you through cultures, religion, or social norms. Over time, you begin to think, feel, and believe that this is the condition of your mind, your body, and your circumstances. Your brain is an organ in your head, and it has limits in its size, **but your mind has no limits**. Let's put this into context: Please close your eyes and, for an instant, imagine you are Superman and can leap out of the atmosphere and travel around the moon and back. It's very simple and very easy—don't listen to your inner monster; just do it.

Welcome back. Now, let's take a tour of the universe, the only way we really can at this moment in time—via the internet. Go to the **www.nasa.gov** web site to see a picture of the universe. Within the search box, type "universe map," and you will be provided different options to select. Find the one that says **"best map ever of the universe NASA."** This picture, will blow your mind; it looks like a gigantic egg with yellow and blue dots. According to scientists, the age of the universe is about 13.75 billion years old. The diameter of the *observable universe* is estimated at around 93 billion light years. Keep in mind that the speed of light is at 186.282 miles per second.

It is so fast that it can go around the earth seven and a half times in one second. As a reminder, a light year is a unit of length equal to approximately 6 trillion miles. The time it would take for light to cross our Milky Way galaxy at the speed of light would be approximately 100,000 years. I understand that this explanation is a little bit complicated, and it is not 100% accurate, but I just want you to understand the point: the universe is much bigger than you imagine.

Within our universe, there are groups of galaxies that form the largest structures in the universe. **Imagine** that you are looking at them on your computer screen, zoom out so you can see them. Our local group, in which our galaxy, the Milky Way, resides, consists of 54 galaxies, and spans approximately 10 million light years from one side of the group to the other. Zoom out some more, and you will see that there is another group called Virgo Supercluster: It has more than 100 groups of galaxies and is approximately 110 million light years from one side to the other. Zoom out even more, and you will see another group of galaxies called Laniakea Supercluster: 100,000 galaxies, 520 million light years to cross them. The Laniakea Supercluster could be one of those yellow dots that you see in the NASA's website map. If you think about all of this, it truly seems that the universe is limitless!

Now, I want you to use your mind and your beliefs to travel through the universe again. Close your eyes, and travel far beyond what we know the universe to be. What does it look like past the reach of our satellites and telescopes? Are there other universes full of galaxies and planets? Or is it a sea of darkness? Chances are, you can only envision darkness, and the reason all comes back to beliefs. Why?

It's because you can't see what you don't believe, and what you believe, you can see. If you believe that another universe exists, you will see it. If you don't believe that another universe exists, you will not see it. **Similarly, if you believe that you will achieve greatness in your life, you will, but if you don't believe it, you won't.** It's that simple. My question for you is this: What do you believe? Look at your life; look at what surrounds you. Do you like what you see? If your answer is yes, then that is perfect; keep doing what you're doing! But if your answer is no, **YOU HAVE TO CHANGE YOUR BELIEFS... NOW.** We've all heard the common phrase, "I'll believe it when I see it," but the reality is that you have to believe it first to be able to see it. The invisible creates the visible. You have to believe it first to be able to achieve it. This is the power of your beliefs. In reality, your beliefs determine who you are.

How Does the Mind Work?

Nobody can argue against the fact that our mind is something unique and powerful. In it, we find many different tools that we can use for our own benefit. Most people do not realize that they have so many tools at their disposal, and if they know they do, they don't understand how they operate. Have you ever heard of the following faculties of your mind?

1. Your conscious mind
2. Your subconscious
3. Your imagination
4. Your thoughts
5. Your reasoning
6. Your memory
7. Your sixth sense
8. Your will
9. Your intuition

10. Your perception
11. Your dreams
12. Your ideas

I'll talk a little bit about all these tools, but I recommend you do a deeper analysis of each of them. Your monster is an expert in ignoring or misusing all these tools, but if you pay attention, your giant will begin to make good use of them, and achieving everything you want in life will be much easier. I would say that almost everyone knows of their conscious mind. Most of the things you do on a daily basis are done consciously: talk, eat, laugh, etc.

If you start asking about what the subconscious is, you will find many people who do not know how to explain what it is, or how it works. Listen to these wise words: **How you think in your subconscious mind is what you manifest into reality.** Our conscious mind consumes a lot of energy. Our subconscious, though, is like autopilot, which allows our mind to save energy by not having to overanalyze and draw conclusions about everything.

Everything we repeat in our conscious mind is repeated several times in our subconscious. For example: "I'm not an intelligent person; therefore, I will never succeed." When you say this in your conscious mind, it's as if you've just confirmed it four times within your subconscious mind. But if you say, "I'm disciplined; therefore, I will learn everything that is necessary to achieve success," this too is recorded several times in your subconscious, and you will achieve it. Your conscious mind gives orders, and your subconscious obeys them all, without asking questions. Make sure the orders your conscious mind is giving are of the most benefit to you.

Now, what can I tell you about the imagination? The **imagination** is the human faculty to represent events, stories, or images of things that do not exist in reality, or that are or were real but are not present. You can use your imagination to plan a vacation or to plan your next business. With imagination, humans have been able to achieve amazing things in the world. Without a doubt, this is one of the tools you have to use first to create the life you want. Sadly, most people, instead of using their imagination to improve their lives, use it against themselves. They imagine the things they do not want, or the problems that may come. But think about it for a minute: If we possess this wonderful faculty, don't you think we are meant to use it for our own betterment, and for the betterment of mankind?

Think about your thoughts; they are like seeds. If you plant a seed in fertile ground, it will grow into a plant—one that could provide food or medicinal properties. **The thoughts of your conscious mind are the seeds, and the fertile soil is your subconscious mind**. Depending on which seed you plant today, will determine the type of crop you will yield in the future. If you do not like the field of crops you have today, you must plant other seeds in your subconscious, in order to cultivate a different, more fruitful crop, and reach your maximum potential.

Re**asoning** is the faculty that allows problem solving, and gives us the ability to gain knowledge and draw our own conclusions about various issues. Animals don't have the ability to reason, but we, as humans, do, and we must use it to our advantage.

Your Giant or Your Monster

Our **memory** is another very important faculty. Of course, we can have fond memories of the past on which to look back and smile, but from the not-so-pleasant memories, we can still learn. Many people don't seem to use their memory at all, and the reason I mention this is because I have seen many people making the same mistakes again and again. We can't torture ourselves for the mistakes of the past, but we do have to learn from them so we don't make the same mistakes again.

We all know of the five senses—hearing, sight, smell, taste, and touch—but the **sixth sense** is the one that most often goes ignored. Just as a person can live without the ability to smell, hear, or see, so too can a person live without using their sixth sense. But when we have and utilize all our senses, life becomes easier—much easier. If you learn to use and trust your sixth sense, you will make better decisions. In the past, I have declined offers to cofound a business or purchase a property, because something just didn't *feel* right about it. Luckily for me, I learned the importance of trusting my own sixth sense because, prior to that, I ended up in a lot of situations that caused me nothing but a headache.

Our **will** is another valuable tool we possess. This is the human capacity to decide freely what you want to do, and what you do not want to do. If you do not like your work, you have the will to change it; if you do not like where you live, you can move. **We can make the decision to let our monster continue to control our life, or we can decide to listen to our giant; it is our free will.**

Our **intuition** is something different. In the United States, I have heard many Americans refer to intuition as a *gut feeling*. It is like

What Tools Can You Use Right Now?

the ability to know, understand, or perceive something clearly and immediately, without the intervention of reason. For example, when you make an important decision and, in your mind, you have many doubts and concerns; but inside, you feel that it is exactly what you should or should not do. Some experts explain that the sixth sense is another word for a person's natural intuition.

Perception is your ability to see, hear, or be aware of something through your senses. Your perception can influence you in a positive or negative way. For example, two people can look at a photo and draw different conclusions, or they can see the same accident occur but explain what happened as if they saw two completely different things. Your perceptions regarding success, life, your country, your families, etc., can help you or stop you, so do an analysis to see if your perceptions are in line with your goals.

What can I say about our **dreams**? I believe that all humans, at least once in their life, have had a dream while sleeping. Other people I know dream often and vividly. But I would like to talk about the ability we all have, to dream while we are awake. If you bought a lottery ticket, maybe you started dreaming about what you would do if you won the prize—how you would give a new car to your wife or husband, or a house to your parents. Or maybe you dreamed about traveling the world or moving to that beautiful beach house. Dreaming is another tool that you have that can profoundly help you to design and plan your life. If you dream of something constantly, it is because you really want it, and I say that if you have the power to dream it, you have the power to make it come true.

Your Giant or Your Monster

Finally, let's talk about **ideas**. To fully understand the power of ideas, you must create them. I challenge you to write three new ideas in the early hours of the morning every day. For example, you may ask yourself: What idea can I use today to do my work faster and more efficiently? How can I improve my business? What idea can I use to improve my friend's business? What idea can I come up with to live a better quality of life? If you see someone complaining about something, come up with an idea to solve that problem. Ask yourself: How can I design another type of plane? How can I improve companies like Amazon or Google? Ask yourself, and try to come up with ideas for everything—even the things that seem on the surface to be hugely successful already. The ideas may seem silly at first, but I assure you that if you're coming up with them, they are needed. And, they may even be quite valuable. Nothing in this world pays more and gives more reward than good ideas. People today will try to convince themselves that everything worthwhile has already been invented, or that they do not have the talent or creativity to conceive new ideas. You and I both know that that is their monster speaking, not their giant.

When you get in the habit of creating new ideas every day, it will be something that your mind will begin to do automatically. You will not believe how many good ideas you will start coming up with. When you get a good idea, remember that you must take action to develop it. If you do not know how, your job will be to find someone who does know, and who can help you. We are the most advanced form of creation. **Some of us choose to use all the tools that we possess in our minds, but most do not.** What will your choice be?

What Tools Can You Use Right Now?

Ask Yourself Better Questions

Our mind is designed to help us achieve the things we want. A few years ago, I learned the importance of asking questions that help our mind find the answer we need. Most people have the habit of asking questions like, "Why don't I have money?" or, "Why do all these bad things happen to me?" and, "Why can't I just be happy?" I could fill this page with questions of this nature, because these are the kinds of questions that our inner monster leads us to ask.

For us to get the answers we really want, we have to ask the right questions. Let me give you an example: Imagine you want to buy your own house, but you have no idea where to start or what to do. You decide to start asking other people. Every time you have the opportunity to ask someone who has already achieved this, your monster asks questions like, "Why can't I buy my own house? Why is it so difficult? How come so many people like me can't buy the house of their dreams?" Undoubtedly, you realize that these would not be the wisest questions to ask if given the opportunity. Instead, if you want to buy a house, and need information, you should look for the right person to guide you, and most likely, you have to look for more than one person.

When your giant finds the right person or people, he asks wise questions like: What is the first step I have to take to be able to buy my house? What are the prices of the houses in this particular area? How much money do I need to have for closing expenses on the day the purchase is made? How much money can the bank lend me based on what I earn? The point is that you have to ask intelligent, thoughtful questions so that you get the answers you need and, ultimately, the steps you will take to see that your goal is achieved.

This goes for more than just purchasing a home. For example: What specific things should I do to lose twenty pounds in six months and not gain them back? What can I start doing today to save more money? What little thing can I start doing today to face the challenges of life with more wisdom and knowledge? Where can I find more like-minded people from whom to learn? What should I change in my life to bring about more peace and happiness? With these specific and wise questions, your mind will lead you to an appropriate answer.

The idea is that, as you discover the appropriate answers that will help you to live a better life, you will be motivated to learn even more. If you create a habit of asking yourself and others these wiser questions, your mind will better seek and recognize the appropriate answers. **I will warn you that your mind will not always give you the answers you want to hear,** for the wiser answers usually require you to be disciplined and take action. But, as we learned in Chapter 5, this is the formula that will lead you to the result you want.

By asking different, better questions, you will find that you receive different, better answers. These answers will stir something inside of you that will make you feel more confident, powerful, energized, and motivated, and will help you remain focused on your desired end result. For as long as you continue to ask the wrong questions, you will continue to get lousy answers that leave you feeling miserable, unmotivated, disappointed, and frustrated. These feelings do not make up ingredients in the recipe for success. If you want that, you need to develop the habit of asking yourself the right questions, which will expose the right answers to your inner giant.

You Have Unlimited Power

I've said it before, and I'll say it again: You are a unique and special person. There is no one else like you on this planet. Although we may look like other people, or have similar characteristics, our behaviors are never exactly like anyone else's. Our minds, while consisting of generally the same organs and functions, are all vastly different, but they do share one common thread—they all have similar potential. Until this moment, you may have never fully considered the power that you have, and that's because, sadly, the majority of people don't believe in themselves, their skills, or their potential, and now you must know why. **Your monster wants to prove to you that you are not good or competent enough to succeed.**

What often happens when we tell a person close to us that we will have our own business, will write a book, will dedicate ourselves to mastering a sport, or that we'll lose weight? Unfortunately, most people respond negatively. They may say it's too hard, you don't have the right work ethic, or that it's not the best time to try for your dreams. Too quickly, we believe them, and continue on in the same routine of our daily lives, trying to forget our goals and accept our lives as they are.

Here's a secret that, if you put it into practice, will change your life completely: ONLY YOU HAVE TO BELIEVE IN YOU—IN YOUR INNER GIANT. Although all these negative things stand out in your mind constantly, BELIEVE IN YOURSELF and in the power of your inner giant, and start working on what you want, little by little. Don't give up! All of your self-doubts may seem valid to you and, in all honesty, the people who know you may, in many cases, have valid reasons not to believe in you either.

Allow me to give you an example: One day, you tell your spouse that you are going to do something extraordinary that you have never done before, like exercising on a daily basis or cleaning out the garage. He or she may laugh in your face. Why? Because they know your way of being and your bad habits. Every day, you get home from work and immediately sit down on the couch with a beer in one hand and the remote in the other, until you fall asleep. On the weekend, it's more of the same. Your spouse never sees you reading or learning new skills, spending time in nature, or straightening up around the house. Thus far, you've shown your spouse that you are not a disciplined or organized person, and chances are that you spend your time with others just like you. That's why, when you tell your spouse that you will accomplish something that is out of character for you, they do not believe you. Sadly, this only contributes to our own lack of belief in ourselves sometimes.

But what if, starting today, you decide that *only you need to believe in you*, and you commit to building your giant for an entire year. During this period, you decide not to waste your time watching pointless television, and you start attending the *university of your own car*, meaning that instead of listening to music while you drive, you listen to successful people through audio books, CDs, or videos from YouTube. Or, perhaps you make the decision not to watch television for a whole year and, instead, start working out, reading, and associating with people who have already achieved what you want to achieve in the

What Tools Can You Use Right Now?

future. When the people that surround you see that you are doing these things, they may have their doubts at first. They might even expect you to eventually give up—which could be a direct reflection of their own habits—but prove them wrong! Over time, they will recognize that you are on the right path, and that you are committed and disciplined, and they will have no choice but to believe in you. Your belief in yourself will only continue to grow as well.

Even though I do not know you, I believe in you. I believe that **the power we possess as human beings has no limits,** and that if you are reading this book, you are trying to discover more about, and to harness, your own power. This is why it is so important that you be wary of the negative thoughts that your monster, and the monster of those around you, will try to infect you with. Every day, you are subjected to negativity, but you must not allow anyone to defeat you when you are trying to achieve something better in your life for you and for others. Remember, **the person who is persistent will triumph.**

Actions to take now:

Take a few minutes and meditate; understand that you have all the tools you need to achieve what you want. Feel the inner power that tells you *"you can,"* even if you have doubts. Write down five affirmations, as a start, and say these out loud to yourself every day. (This drives your monster crazy!) Use words that resonate with you. Examples are: "I *can* do it," or, "I *do* believe in me," or, "My power is *limitless*." Your beliefs will make the difference. What will you believe about yourself from now on? Write it. Go to www.buildingyourgiant.com/bonuses to gain access to exclusive content on the website and be able to view or download a list of affirmations.

What Tools Can You Use Right Now?

Notes

Chapter 7

What Is Your Giant's Code of Honor?

"A person without a code of honor is like a car without a motor."
– Josue Lopez

Is Your Word a Contract?

In this world, you can find both men and women who have an outstanding code of honor. Yet there are also many who don't even know what a code of honor is. Being the success-minded person you must be, to be reading this book, you will need to know what your code of honor is, and what it means to you, and be in the habit of automatically living by it.

Simply put, a code of honor is a standard of behavior regarded as proper. It is important to analyze yourself to determine if your code of honor matches the person you wish to become. I also advise being mindful of the people around you. Those who are controlled by their inner monster don't believe that having an excellent honor code is vital.

Your Giant or Your Monster

By this point, you have committed to letting your inner giant be in control, and one of the most outstanding character traits of your giant is being trustworthy, which means living by an excellent code of honor. Trust that in order to become extraordinary in every aspect of your life, an excellent code of honor is necessary. Ask yourself: *Do I feel satisfied with my code today, or do I want to improve or refine it?*

I already mentioned that small things that seem insignificant are often the most important. Maybe you don't think that keeping your word all the time is important, especially for *insignificant* things, but remember, it's all about demonstrating, at all times, that you are guided by your inner giant, not your monster.

Your giant makes and keeps promises, big and small, to others and to yourself. If you say things to yourself, such as, "Today, I'm going to eat healthy all day. I'll go to the gym for an hour, and then I'll spend some quality time with my family," then keep your word, and **do it**.

Don't forget to take one step at a time. Follow through with doing the first thing you said you would. *Consider your words as a contract with yourself.* By not breaking this contract, you will demonstrate to yourself, and others, that you are guided by your inner giant. **This will be the foundation of your code of honor.** Once you've taken the first step and laid the foundation for your honor code, you can continue to build on it by contracting with yourself to achieve other tasks and goals.

I know from experience that it is sometimes easier to keep our word when dealing with others, but much more of a challenge to keep it when we deal with ourselves. I'm telling you now, you

What Is Your Giant's Code of Honor?

cannot let this happen. Let your giant take control, not the monster. Once you have your code of honor established, you will be more aware of what you say to yourself and to others. You will also learn to be more mindful of the commitments you choose to make. When you begin to consider your word a contract, you may find that you have to learn to say **no** to a lot of things. You no longer will make a promise just because it is easier in the moment to be agreeable, even when you have serious doubts that you will keep that promise. It may feel hard at first, but that is just your monster trying to claw its way back into the driver's seat.

Another drawback of saying *yes* when your inner giant is shaking its head *no*, is that you overpromise to others and end up neglecting your own priorities. For me, this was a big problem, as I was afraid to say no, which meant I was always busy solving other people's problems because I always kept my word. I didn't have time to do the most important things for me, until one day, I decided to start saying NO.

The reaction from those around me was mixed. Many said to me, "You have changed so much, I don't even know you." By saying no, I gave people the opportunity to learn to deal with their own problems—whether they wanted to or not. Humans have a natural tendency to dump their problems onto others, and we also have a tendency to take those problems on to solve, because they seem easier than dealing with our own. But with this constant game of give and take, no one is given the opportunity to learn to solve their own problems. Personal growth occurs every time we endeavor to solve our own problems, which happens to be bad news for our monster within, who wants us to stay weak and lazy. This robs us of the opportunity for growth, and hinders us from building our self-confidence and self-esteem. If you act like someone's monster, and treat them as if they are too weak to solve their own problems, you are robbing them of the opportunity for growth.

Soon after being reminded by my giant that I needed to say yes to my own priorities, my conversations with those seeking my help evolved. When I'd suggest that someone make a phone call to obtain information they were seeking, they would ask for me to call for them, since I "knew what to say." Instead of putting their problem on my plate, I would politely tell them that making their call for them would do them no favors. It would not help them grow, and the truth was that I was already very busy (even if I was busy catching up on much-needed rest). Now, don't get me wrong; I'm not saying that you should stop helping others. After considering a person's request, it may be the proper thing to do, if it could be done without disempowering them. I only want you to keep in mind that if you say you're going to do something, do it. And, if you sense that they should do this for themselves, or you have any doubts about being able to keep your word, it is okay to say **no.**

Follow through on your word, and you will grow as a person, surrounded by other honorable people. Opportunities will come along, simply because you will be recognized as a person who can be trusted. Nobody wants to do business with someone who is unreliable or lies, so be different. Show the world that your word is a contract that you never break.

What Is Your Giant's Code of Honor?

Can Other People Trust You?

I want you to think of a person that you know you trust fully. Maybe it's a very close relative or maybe a friend. How do you know you can trust this person? What is it that sets them apart? You may be thinking: *I have known him/her for a long time; he/she has shown me that he/she will not betray me; he/she has great values; he/she is admired and respected by everyone; he/she keeps his/her word*, and so on.

Trust is interesting because it takes time to develop—in many cases, years—but in just a moment, it can be lost. I've had friendships with people that I once admired and helped on many occasions, but over time, some of these friends began to make choices that didn't align with my core values. They began making selfish decisions, thinking of their own benefit no matter the consequence for others. It began to be painful to witness. I had to make the decision to separate myself from these people, my former friends, before they hurt me.

Trust is extremely valuable, and being able to trust a person is an important quality. Others should **know that you can be trusted** to never betray them in any way. This applies to your family, friendships, and in your business. When you establish this level of trust, people genuinely want the best for you, and they do what they can to help you, just as you help them.

Learn to say no, but when you say yes, remember that **your word is a contract**. Therefore, you must comply with the terms. If you try to back out, or tell others that you forgot or simply got too busy, those people will lose confidence in you, and word will spread. Now, I understand that sometimes life gets in the way, and things come up that may require us to put our prior commitment on hold. This is why it is even more important that, if you have an agreement that you can't meet, you communicate with the other party directly and clearly. Tell him or her specifically why you are not able to keep your word as planned, and what your new promise is, and how you will fulfill this contract. You have to do this at the moment you know that you are not going to be able to comply with the agreement—not a week, six months, or a year later. Doing this simple task will further build your foundation of trust with others. It may seem like common sense, but I assure you that for most, it is not. Why do you think that is?

The answer is simple: The monster that we have inside is a lazy coward, and what it does is run and hide instead of following through on agreements that start to feel inconvenient or burdensome. This is the opposite of being strong and brave, and living by a code of honor.

Maybe you would not dare to betray a person in your business, or a friend, but what if you betray your spouse? In my opinion, if you are willing to betray your partner in life, it is only a matter of time before you will betray others; by that time, your monster is in full control. Many will stop trusting you, **and worse, you will know that you can't even trust yourself.** Your inner monster is always looking for the opportunity to take control of your life. Don't let him.

You may not have realized it before, but this one way in which you may have let your monster be in control at times, could be why you are not doing as well in life as you would like. If you do not face your problems, or follow through on your commitments, no matter how much you may dread them, and instead choose to run or hide, you are only holding yourself back. You, as well as other people, start to believe that you cannot be trusted. Others will keep you at a distance because of your flaky behavior, and for good reason. Instead of doors of opportunity opening to you, they will stay shut because you are too much of a risk.

You are reading this book because you want to learn something new and be able to improve your life, so let this be one of the many critical lessons you will learn here: Keeping your word, even in the smallest of ways, is important. Just the fact that people can trust you will help you change your life completely. And every time you honor your word, you feed the giant within you, making him strong and in control, which is your number one goal.

I'll tell you something else: When you trust yourself, and when others can trust you, the result is an inner peace that cannot be compared to anything else. Anywhere you go, you will find open doors instead of closed ones. But remember, that is not a matter of working for a few days to build trust, and then giving up on it. Trust takes time and effort to build, but it is easy to lose—so this trustworthy person is the person to strive to be now, today, and every day for the rest of your life. As you keep your commitment to let your giant be in control, you will live as a person that others can trust, and as someone who lives by an excellent code of honor.

Are You a Person of Integrity?

Being a person of integrity is very important and involves many character traits, like being an honest person. Undoubtedly, these two words are related, but I want to highlight the fact that there is a difference between being an honest person and being a person with integrity. In many circumstances, being an honest person is difficult; however, not being so always costs you. Every day, you should be striving to be a better version of yourself than you were yesterday. When you live as a dishonest person, you demonstrate to others, and to society as a whole, that you are a corrupt person. If you have no compelling desire to be an honest person, you are not transforming for the better, but rather for the worse, in front of and in the minds of those around you.

To be honest with yourself and other people, you need courage, and the higher the values you have, the more honesty you can demonstrate. Honesty protects you in many ways, even if you don't believe it. Yokoi Kenji said it perfectly: **"Honesty is precious, but integrity is essential."** Honesty speaks of what you **do** on the outside, what you **say** to others, and of how you **deal** with all the people around you. Every person in the world knows that we have to be honest when dealing with others. When a person is not honest, others quickly mark them as someone they cannot trust.

Being a person with integrity goes beyond that. Yokoi further stated: **"Integrity involves who you really are inside."** So, now I ask you: *Who are you on the inside?* I wrote this book to help you understand yourself. It's why I asked: *Are you a person of integrity?* Perhaps you are portraying on the outside someone or something that is not true to who you really are. Is your outer behavior congruent with your inner character? You may be asking yourself if it's even possible to live life in such a way, and the answer is *yes*. You can show people and tell people all you want about the life you dream of having, but when nobody is watching you, are you following the example of those who have already achieved the great things you desire? Are you living in an honest manner, and with integrity?

Let me give you an example: To those around me, I can pretend that I'm a religious person and that I accept and agree with all the doctrines of my religion. Perhaps I even visit church with my family on a weekly basis. But now, let's talk about my **integrity—what I am on the inside**. Maybe I don't believe in the Bible as the word of God, and I don't follow its teachings. I get drunk every night, and I cheat on my wife. Maybe I disagree with religion in general, and feel that the doctrines they have for people are ridiculous. Maybe I go to church because I don't want to be judged or criticized by others, or because my family forces me. To others, I seem one way, but I know that on the inside, I am very different.

I hope you understand the point—you can pretend on the outside, but inside, you can't hide anything from your soul.

To be able to achieve everything you want in this life, you have to know and understand the importance of having integrity in the deepest part of yourself, especially when no one else is around. This must become part of your code of honor, striving to do the right thing all the time. In this world, not everything will go exactly as you want, as nothing and no one is perfect. *But if you can count on yourself to always do the right thing, others will learn they can also count on you.* Your inner monster doesn't want to know anything about honesty and integrity, but with these essential qualities, your inner giant will continue to grow and become powerful, to the point of feeling invincible. Doesn't that sound great?

> *"Moral excellence comes about as a result of habit. We become just by doing just acts, temperate by doing temperate acts, brave by doing brave acts."*
> – Aristotle

Are You Brave?

Anyone can be brave, but many people choose not to be, because it is easier to be a coward. There is far less effort involved. However, to be able to accomplish bigger things in life, you must be brave. I want you to know that your giant is very brave, but the main reason why he does not take action most of the time is because your monster is holding him back. You have to let your giant come out and do something he has never done before. Successful people are brave because they are willing to do just that.

Everyday life is full of decisions to make, some with huge potential, some of little consequence. Bring your courage to every single decision, big or small. To make the decision to opt out of watching a TV show with someone because you are drawn to finishing the inspiring book you are reading instead, you have to be **brave;** to invest time and money to attend a seminar for self-improvement, you need to be **brave**; to start your own business, you must be **brave.** If you know someone who is full of wisdom or has attained great knowledgeable, that took being **brave**. To become a wealthy person, you have to be **brave**.

What Is Your Giant's Code of Honor?

When you think of someone for whom you have great admiration, know that they had to be **brave** along the way to succeed at what they have achieved. The speaker in front of a large audience had to be brave just to learn anything about speaking in public, and to give it a try. If you are a member of a club where you can learn to speak in public (like Toastmasters International), you must be very **brave**. Most people say they are more afraid to speak in public than of death. If this is one of your biggest fears, and you manage to overcome it, you will be unstoppable. To become an extraordinary human being, you have to be **brave.**

Most people don't like change; they always want to stay in their comfort zone. Let me give you an example: Imagine that you have an elegant and expensive boat, one with outboard motors, like a Contender, Intrepid, or Yellowfin, and it is parked at your house on top of a new trailer. Every day, you look at it, but you never put it in the water or take it to the open sea. What a waste that would be! Your inner giant is just like that elegant boat. Don't let it waste away in dry dock, under control of your monster. Instead, be **brave,** and set it free so you can grow and explore every aspect of your life.

It is true that the most revered and timeless stories are those about brave men and women. Much has been written about the brave, not only for what they have been able to accomplish for themselves, but for what they have been able to do for others. That is why every time you are faced with being courageous, you must do it. The more courage you have, the greater your chances for finding success and living the excellent life you dream of. And you will be in a better position to help others.

117

I went on vacation with my family to the Dominican Republic, and while we were there, we went to visit a place called El Hoyo Azul. When we arrived, we were welcomed by the beauty of a brilliantly blue natural spring. A tall, wooden deck had been built around the spring, from which visitors could jump into the water. My son was eight years old at that time, and wanted to jump, but he had not yet found the courage. For about five minutes, he stood looking over the edge, creeping closer, then moving away, then moving closer again. Spectators began to cheer him on, encouraging him to jump until, finally, he had enough courage to do so. Can you guess what happened after his first jump? He wanted to do it again and again!

The same feelings of fear and apprehension occur to people of all ages, in all sorts of scenarios. People want to try something new, and accomplish great things, but they don't have the courage. Their fear controls them and holds them down; in many cases, for a lifetime. But do you know what happens when you find the courage and do whatever it is that you've been too afraid to try? You become braver, and those things that you were once scared to death about become a lot easier. Your confidence grows, as your inner giant is strengthened, too. And if at first you don't succeed when you try something new, don't let it stop you. Continue to be brave, and try, try again.

Are You an Organized Person?

Ask yourself: In what area of my life do I need to be more organized? What are the benefits? Why is it so important? Where do I begin? The moment you decide to organize your life and surroundings, you become a better person, with a much higher probability of great success. I know many people who are not organized, and this has stopped them in their tracks, while others who are organized zoom by them.

Disorganization is a handicap, and it can be compared to walking in mud: You move forward, but with every step you take, your feet get buried bit by bit, requiring a lot of strength and effort to raise your foot in order to take another step. If you want to keep moving at a good pace toward your goals, you must get organized in all areas of your life. Otherwise, your personal environment will become like quicksand, and it will be harder and harder to gain any traction.

Your inner monster doesn't feel the urgency to get organized. To him, it is unimportant, and he prefers to leave everything for tomorrow. However, your giant is the opposite. He does not want to leave anything for tomorrow; he wants to do everything today. After all, tomorrow is something none of us are promised. So, where do you think you should begin to get better organized? I suggest starting with your **mind** first, then **organize your emotions, then your body, and lastly** your **surroundings**. It is very difficult to organize anything in the exterior of your life, if you do not organize your interior first. We will discuss this more, a little later in the book.

One of the wisest and most practical suggestions that I can give you is: **ONE THING AT A TIME, BUT WITH PERSISTENCE.** If you start organizing your office, for example, do it one piece of paper at a time. Pick it up, and don't set it down until it is in its rightful place—especially if it belongs in the trash. Do the same thing at home, one item at a time. You may have seen **FOCUS** defined as **Following One Course Until Successful**. When you focus on handling one thing at a time, but

Your Giant or Your Monster

with persistence, you will be successful in your goal of becoming organized.

Listen to this wise, practical advice that I learned the hard way: **WHEN YOU LOSE, SOMETIMES, YOU WIN A LOT.** Let me explain how this advice can be applied in many areas of life. When you look at your garage or your house, who would you guess is in charge, your monster or your giant? You can tell at a glance, right? In many cases, garages are full of everything except cars. If yours is full of possessions, hold a garage sale and sell everything you are not using. Whatever you can't sell, give away, and whatever is left, throw away. Don't get caught up on how much money you spent on something that you may now be giving or throwing away. Stay focused on getting organized, because this will always make it easier for your inner giant to be in control.

Chances are that if things have been stored out in the garage, it's because you don't need them in your life. The more things you have in your life that you don't need, the more burden you carry, and the less you can relax. Remember, we don't need a lot of things to survive, and a simple life can be even more enjoyable. I think that having a few things of high value is better than having a lot of worthless junk. Would you agree?

This leads me to another point. If you find yourself in possession of a lot of unnecessary things, maybe you and your family are being guided by the emotions at a given moment, and buying things you don't really need. Learn the lesson, and save more money so that you can invest in something more productive. If your economic life is disorganized, then put into practice what you will learn later in this book, so that you can organize yourself

What Is Your Giant's Code of Honor?

and have control over your money, too.

Wanting to keep many unnecessary things is the idea of the inner monster, for he is always thinking about survival and not about creating. He always feels that he will need all those things someday. This is the mentality of poor people, not rich people. The more organized your life is, the easier it will be for your giant to focus on the things of value, and to enjoy life. Keep your life simple.

Always simplify before you attempt to get organized. Whether at home or at your company office, isn't it easier to organize 400 things instead of 4,000 things? And then, once you have simplified and organized what you choose to keep, you must commit to staying on top of it. Once organized does not mean forever organized, unless you maintain it. One of the best ways to prevent chaos from creeping back in is to create systems for you and your family, so that everyone has a role and everything stays organized. A home system can be as simple as: *When mom or dad arrives home after grocery shopping, son and/or daughter will go out to the car and bring in all the bags of groceries, no matter how many trips it takes. Meanwhile, mom or dad will unpack and put everything in its place.* This is a *system*, because it is a procedure that everyone can learn to follow, and the frequency is *as needed*. Anything that includes a series of tasks that gets repeated, should be turned into a system, and followed, in order to maintain an organized environment.

Do You Help Others?

Within your code of honor, there must be a passion for helping others improve their lives. You have to feel the desire in your heart to see that other people also thrive. You must pay attention to this because, if your inner monster has his way, you'll be focused only on yourself. Your monster is greedy and craves all material possessions and recognition. He is always thinking about the **I**. Is it any coincidence that today's world is consumed with **I**—iPhone, iPod, iPad, I want, I need, etc.?

If the inner monster is always thinking of the **self**, and most of the people around us are controlled by the internal monster, that explains why the tendency of most people is to think about themselves, not others, at all times. Even when they see that others are working hard and thriving, they are envious or unhappy to see others succeeding.

If you have ever felt this way, I can tell you that your inner monster is to blame. **People who are dominated by their giant, commit to achieve success in everything they do, while also helping others succeed, and then rejoice when that success is reached.** These people understand that there are plenty of riches in the world. There is no need for poverty, or "for me to win, you must lose," when greatness can be achieved by all.

Your inner monster, on the other hand, only sees scarcity in the world, and he focuses on this scarcity all the time. The idea that there is not enough for everyone is your monster mentality, but I want you to trust and believe that Earth has everything we need to be able to enjoy life to the fullest. And I, for one, want the good people of the world to live a life full of wealth and abundance. I'd love to look around and see healthy, happy people walking around clean, well-kept cities, lined with beautiful houses full of comforts, with luxurious cars parked in the driveways. For this to happen, though, we must all focus on helping others.

This leads me to another secret for achieving everything you want in life, faster: **Focus on providing a service of some kind that benefits others.** The more people you can serve and help, the sooner you will achieve what you want. It's that simple. People who have developed great inventions, such as electricity, computers, telephones, airplanes, etc., have changed the world because they have helped millions. Not only have you and I benefited from these inventions, but by helping so many others, the inventors themselves benefited as well.

Perhaps at this moment, you do not have a million-dollar idea that can change the world, **but any service that you are able to provide to others can still be life changing and life improving.** Is there a way you can make it even more effective and more far-reaching?

If you have a restaurant, you could come up with new methods of feeding more people, by speeding up your processes or expanding your space. If you have rental properties, consider how you can manage more properties in order to provide more homes to other people. If you paint, think about how you can bring more beauty to the world by painting more houses, cars, or buildings. If you provide employment to five people, see if you can expand and add positions so you can employ ten or more. If you work for another person, and you do not have the opportunity to serve many people, but you want to, then maybe it is time to start thinking about having your own company. **Serving more people, and helping them get what they want or need, is the key to achieving everything you want—quickly.** But, to better serve and help others, you have to first become better yourself.

Actions to take now:

Write your code of honor in a paragraph or two. If you already had your code of honor before reading this book, then examine it for areas of improvement. If you never thought of your own honor code before, write it clearly. Be specific so you know and understand the set of values, character traits, and behaviors that will define you from now on.

What Is Your Giant's Code of Honor?

Notes

Chapter 8

Can You Control What You Feel?

*"Your feelings and emotions can serve you,
and they can also enslave you."*
– Josue Lopez

Fear: Is It Friend or Foe?

Does fear dominate you, or do you control it? To control your fears, first you have to understand them. Fear is your best friend, and it is also your worst enemy. Let me explain: Today, you are alive, fed, clothed, and reading this book—thanks to your fears. Fear is something natural. It is the one thing that tells you where the dangers are so you can avoid them and continue to survive. If you are at the top of a building, your fears warn you that if you slip over the edge, the landing will be quite painful and will probably result in your death. If you are near water that is swarming with great white sharks, your fear will keep you from jumping in because of the danger that exists.

Yes, fear protects you, but fear will also bind and prevent you from trying new things. For example, if you have to speak in public, even when you are prepared, your nerves, or your monster in this case, make you feel like you are going to die. In reality, even if everything goes wrong during your speech, and people laugh or criticize you, the act of speaking in public will not kill you. Your ego may end up battered and bruised, and sometimes the fear of that is enough to keep you from taking the risk and stepping outside of your comfort zone.

Think of a roller coaster, or many of the other attractions that you can find at amusement parks. You trust that these are safe and that nothing bad will happen if you ride them, so you get on them and enjoy the ride. Why do they still seem so scary? Because our fear does not sleep; it always wants to protect us and, yes, sometimes drives us crazy in the process. But eventually, when we get past the worry and conquer the fear, we realize that it "wasn't so bad," and that we are still alive to tell about the adventure. So, while it's perfectly normal to feel fear, don't let it run—or ruin—your life.

In order to grow as a person, we have to make the decisions to act, even if we feel fear. If we do not act when we feel fear, we will not achieve personal freedom. *Fear keeps you focused on the past and concerned about the future.* Sometimes we feel fear for things that never happen, but the biggest fear we should have is the fear of never having lived. I want you to remember that if you are not willing to do new things, then there will be many things in life that you will never explore, learn, or enjoy—not because you had fear, but because you decided to let it control you.

Keep in mind that we do not have control of the outside world, but we can have control of our inner world. So, do something that scares you every day, to grow as a person. This is the only way to control your fears. Fear is like the air we need to keep us alive, but when the air is blowing out of control because of a storm, it can be deadly. Do not hate your fears, because they are part of who you are, and you need them—just do not let them control you.

What if I tell you that on the road to success, fear is your GPS (Global Positioning System)? The GPS is a prime example of an invention that has changed the world. If you own a phone, you probably have this tool at your fingertips, literally. You can travel around the world without worrying about getting lost. Simply enter your desired destination, and the GPS easily guides you there, turn by turn. Let me explain now how your fear, acting as your GPS, can also guide you to your desired destination on the road to success: Each action that triggers fear is likely the exact action you need to take in order to grow and achieve the next level of success in life.

If you are afraid to speak in public, then this is what you have to do. If you are afraid to talk to a new client, then that is precisely what you have to do. If you are afraid to apologize for a mistake you made, that is exactly what you have to do. If you want to start your own business, but you are afraid of failure, that is very likely what you have to do. Also, in your personal life, notice where fear is stopping you. If you want to ask a particular person to go out on a date with you, but you are afraid, that is precisely what you have to do. Don't let your inner monster or fear of rejection stop you.

The presence of fear is indicating to you that it is time to act; follow these turn-by-turn directions.

Can You Control Your Emotions?

We all know people who cannot face their own life. They opt for temporary fixes such as: *When I'm sad, I turn to sweets. When I'm nervous, it helps to smoke a cigarette. When I feel stressed, I calm down with alcohol. When I'm depressed, I hide away in my room. When I feel anxiety or despair, I numb the pain with drugs. When I'm angry, I get physically aggressive. To feel happy, I need money. To feel peace, I need to go on vacation.* These provide hollow, short-term solutions, at best. Usually, the problems only get worse when these strategies are used.

Without a doubt, we all experience different emotions, and depending on the day, sometimes these emotions can range from extremely joyful to extremely sad, angry, or anxious. We are human, and this is a completely normal part of life, but for the majority of people, those controlled by their inner monster, the negative emotions are the ones they feel most often.

As you have already made the decision to be a person controlled by your inner giant, you must understand that you need to have control over what you feel, and how you react to it. If your current vices include smoking, using drugs, or drinking too much alcohol, it is evident that your monster is controlling you. From now on, you must take control of your body. You tell your body what it needs to do, not the other way around. Not having control of oneself is a great sign of weakness. **Many people, today, know that regaining control of themselves is exactly what they have to do, yet they do not do it.**

Everything you wish to do in life always begins with a decision—a clear and firm decision. Sometimes these decisions will lead you down a better path; sometimes they won't. I know several people who wish to quit smoking, but they tell me they can't because it's just too difficult. Imagine right now if you were to decide never to smoke again, no matter what. Would you die? Of course not! If anything, it could have the opposite effect of prolonging your life.

I have other friends who, on many occasions, have made big and important money decisions, like buying an expensive car or a new boat. The bad decision was not the purchase of the car or boat itself, as much as the decision to do so despite their poor financial standing. We all buy things that we want and may not need, but if, for example, someone is struggling to keep a roof over their head, it probably isn't the best time to purchase a boat—unless they plan to live on it.

Why do so many people make decisions of this kind when they know that what they are doing is unintelligent and irresponsible? Because they continue to let themselves be controlled by their inner monster. In other words, they are letting themselves be controlled by what they feel at the moment, without thinking about the consequences that their decisions will have in the future.

Listen to this, and never forget: **EVERY DECISION—SMALL OR LARGE—THAT YOU MAKE TODAY MATTERS BECAUSE IT WILL AFFECT YOU—FOR BETTER OR FOR WORSE—IN THE FUTURE.** This is why controlling what you feel is essential, so that by making smarter, more responsible decisions, you can ensure a better quality of life down the road.

Regardless of whether you believe in the Bible as the word of God or man, it holds valuable lessons. *"I discipline my body and make it my slave."* From these words, as found in 1 Corinthians 9:27, we can understand the importance of learning to control our own bodies and the power it can yield. If you are not already familiar with this habit, it may seem difficult at first, but it is something you must learn to do to grow as a person. If you cannot control yourself, it will be much harder to control external things.

It's easy to give in to your body when you let it control you. Eating whatever you want, buying expensive things, smoking, drinking, or being unfaithful to your partner—all of these may provide instant gratification, but it is short-lived. The true, long-term gratification comes when you take control of yourself. In the wise words of Zig Ziglar, *"If you will be hard on yourself, life will be easy on you. But if you insist upon being easy on yourself, life is going to be very hard on you."* Now is the time to start making the smart and responsible decisions to put yourself back in control. You will soon see how your life changes for the better.

What Is Your Definition of Failure?

Failure is one of the best teachers we can all have. For many, it is difficult to understand how failure can be beneficial at all, because it's often quite difficult to experience and accept. However, winners will tell you that failure does not exist; what exists is a result. If you do not get your desired result, you should try again, using a different approach. A simple definition of failure is: An adverse outcome to an event or occurrence that was expected to go well.

Can You Control What You Feel?

Let me give you an example: If you set out on a new diet and follow the instructions, but you find that after a period of time you are not achieving the results you had hoped and worked for, you may feel that you have failed. The truth is that while you did not get your desired result, you have not failed at all. Instead of giving up all together, the wise thing for you to ask yourself is why this specific diet is not working for you. You could even turn to an expert, such as a nutrition coach or personal trainer, to assist you. The important thing to remember in this scenario is that there are many reasons why a person cannot lose weight. It's not always as simple as eating fewer calories and exercising more.

Imagine that the result you wish to achieve is the top of a mountain, and there are many paths you can take to reach it. Some may be shorter and more treacherous, while others may take longer but provide a smoother climb. If you falter on one, it does not mean you are a failure and cannot or should not make another attempt, but in the process, you are learning which route may be best for you. The fear of failure will stop most people, especially people who are controlled by their monster, but it will never stop people who are controlled by their inner giant.

You only fail when you give up.

When you do not get the result you want, your monster wants you to feel as though you have already failed, and should, therefore, give up. *He wants you to prove to yourself that you are not competent enough, or that you are not intelligent enough.* Never give him the pleasure of seeing you defeated. Another example could be when you start a business, and it does not work as expected, or it does not result in the profits you thought, and goes bankrupt. As with weight loss, there are many reasons why a business may be unsuccessful, and you must look at the whole picture to determine why. Instead of automatically blaming yourself and labeling yourself a failure, analyze why your business did not provide the result you had hoped and expected it would. Could it be that your location was not suitable for attracting new customers, or that your prices weren't competitive enough? Maybe there simply wasn't a market for the goods or services you were offering. Rather than throw in the towel and go back to working for someone else, take what you learned and make changes to your existing operations, or try something new to be more successful in your next business endeavor. This is very important; don't find people to blame. If you point the finger you will not learn anything; take personal responsibility and remember that considering yourself to be nothing but a failure will never result in being a success.

Your inner giant has a very different attitude about failure than you may realize. Here is a perfect example of someone who obviously has been living with her inner giant in control: Sara Blakely. She was America's first female, self-made billionaire, in her 20s! In an interview, she revealed what her inner giant thinks about the fear of failure:

"I grew up in a house where my father encouraged my brother and me to fail. I specifically remember coming home and saying, 'Dad, Dad, I tried out for this or that, and I was horrible,' and he would high-five me and say, 'Way to go'...He actually encouraged us to fail. At the dinner table, he would ask us what we failed at that week. If we didn't have something, he would be disappointed. It changed my mindset at an early age that failure is not the outcome—failure is not trying. Don't be afraid to fail."

Can You Control What You Feel?

I have not ever heard any person who has triumphed in a big way say that they didn't have to face some kind of failure along the way. It is part of life; it is part of the price that is paid in most cases. There is no doubt that when things do not go as planned, and you spend all of your time, energy, and money on something that doesn't succeed, it hurts—a lot. It also hurts when you think about the people who were involved, who supported you or worked with and for you, who did not get to share in a success either. Trust me, I know from experience how painful it is to think of your family and how the world you had hoped to give them seems to be further from your reach than ever.

I want to emphasize that you should not feel like a failure, because that was not your plan. Your plan, if it was honest and ethical, should have given you success. Think about what you learned, and try again. In the United States, there are seemingly infinite opportunities to start over. True, it may not be the case for all areas of the world, but I mention it to you because it's like being given a second or third chance to the people who are striving to succeed. And when a person triumphs, everyone around them benefits.

You never plan to fail, but many often let the fear of failure prevent them from even trying. People who are guided by their giant are never stopped by such fear. Winners at life know that there is no shortage of opportunities. The winners know that the mind controls the body, so they let their giant take control of their life. In the game of baseball, if you do not play often, you will probably strike out instead of hitting a homerun, but you cannot give up. If you are playing soccer and miss scoring a goal, and you lose the game, you cannot give up. The road to success is a series of games, some of which are lost. Those who ultimately walk away with the best record are those who are not afraid to fail, who always strive to improve, and **who approach each new game as if they are already the victors.**

Different Personalities

When you sit down to analyze humankind, you quickly realize that we are all very different. Not only do we all look different, but we also have different personalities. Our actions and choices in different situations can also be very different. Have you ever found yourself wondering why someone acted in a specific way? Maybe it was the opposite of how you would have handled something. The reality is that we all tend to act according to our way of thinking, and according to the way we see life. In my experience, I have encountered three common groups within which people can be categorized.

Comfort seekers comprise the first group. A person in this group may own an expensive car—a Ferrari. Every day, they go out to their car, which is parked in the garage; they open the garage, start the engine, and push down hard on the accelerator. Over and over, they rev up the engine as the garage fills with smoke, and the walls around them begin to vibrate, shaking the hanging tools to the ground. After a few minutes, they shut off the car and walk back into the house, where they resume sitting in their favorite comfortable chair. This first group never actually removes their car from the garage—ever.

This first group of people is the group that is so controlled by their fears that they **never** leave their comfort zone. They take no risks and never try anything new because they do not want to fail, which prevents them from ever living the life that they really want to live. This type of person is common in the world today. They have great potential; they may have amazing opportunities, but they usually also have a thousand excuses to justify avoiding that potential and those opportunities.

If you invite them to attend a seminar where they can learn something new, they will tell you that it's not necessary, that they know enough. If you talk about starting a business, they tell you they do not have the start-up funds. If you advise them to look for a better job, they tell you there are no jobs available out there or there are too many other candidates to contend with. If you show them how to establish a new company using a business model that has already been proven, they will tell you that it is too late. If you tell them to do something to help other people, they will tell you that they do not have time. This first group is always full of excuses to never have to do anything of importance for themselves or for others.

Usually, they get carried away by the emotions of the moment, and make the same mistake time after time, which prevents them from advancing in any way. They waste their valuable time with bad habits, like watching a lot of television, playing video games, or hanging out on social media—all in the comfort of their own comfortable chair, in their familiar space. They are unproductive and get by in life focusing on things that do not matter, while finding the negative in everything. They are an exact demonstration of when a person is controlled by the internal monster. They have no control of themselves, so they live a mediocre or even miserable life, never risking enough to leave their personal comfort zone.

The second group are the "fast-laners." A typical fast-laner drives a Lamborghini. Unlike the first group, this group member backs their car out of their garage, pushes the accelerator to the floorboard, and never lets up. These people live in the fast lane and do whatever is necessary to get what they want. If you are in their way, they will run you right over. You may ask these people: *Are you able to devote time to your spouse, children, friends, and other relatives? Do you find time to eat healthy and exercise? Are you enjoying the ride of life and all the beautiful scenery that the planet has to offer along the way?* Their answer: "No, who has time for any of that in the fast lane? The only way to achieve more is to constantly be on the move. Bye!" These people zoom through life and forget to explore and enjoy every aspect of it.

Their focus is always on reaching that thing that they do not yet have, thinking that with IT, happiness will be found. For these people, their actual quality of life, their family or friends, are not important. They worship money like a god but never have inner peace or satisfaction because they think that happiness is in material possessions.

These people are often surrounded by luxury and wealth. They live in mansions, but the mansion is enjoyed only by their dogs. They think that as long as they stay in the fast lane, they will live forever—so even though they reach old age, they do not stop working, always wanting more and more. They give nothing back or give very little. Their plans to have more never change, because only in the achievements do they find momentary satisfaction, which soon wears off and points them over the next hill, around the next corner…with no time given to enjoying the present.

Can You Control What You Feel?

To be able to build wealth, in most cases, requires making great sacrifices for a few years, but the problem is that in this group of people, it becomes their way of living. They sacrifice the gift of the present, and they rush off, often sacrificing their own health as well as peace of mind. They never develop and use their own wisdom. They do not realize that in order to change this way of being, they need to get out of that routine for a while, to reprogram their mind and enjoy what they have achieved. This group of people never finds balance, and for this reason, we listen to the stories of people who, despite having everything in a material sense, even fame, take their own lives, or suffer from depression or substance abuse addiction.

They strive a lifetime to be part of that small percentage of humanity that is very, very rich, as if this were the most important thing. They do not realize that life is simple and wonderful, that we are on this planet only for a short while, and that the most important things are not material things but are found within oneself and in the family and good friendships that surround us. These people lose balance in their lives to the point of not loving themselves and never knowing what it is to feel true peace in their souls.

I call the third group the Giants, and I bet you can guess why. A person in this group drives a Bentley and is not afraid to take it out of their garage. They step on the gas to catch some speed because they are not afraid to overcome their fears, but they obey the speed limit and slow down or yield to others, as any courteous driver would do.

These people take care of their bodies every day by eating healthy and exercising. They slow down and park their bodies and minds often, in order to spend time with their families and friends, making sure every day to enjoy the journey of life, because they know that they will only live once and have to enjoy the ride.

This group of people lets themselves be guided by their inner giant. They focus on things of value, things that really matter. They have significant purpose in their life; they also have goals and are very disciplined. They strive to have more time and money to devote to doing things that have value for humanity. They are people who always focus on the positive things in life. These people are always thinking about improving their lives and the lives of others. They are very connected to their life and to who they are inside.

These people know what it is to give, without expecting anything in return. They act with wisdom; they take time to meditate, and they learn something new and useful every day. Their plans are concrete and solid, with significant objectives in mind. These are the people we all want to have in our lives, not only because they always exhibit a positive attitude, but because you can trust them. If they pulled up and said, "Hop in!" you would go along with no hesitation, because you know them to be sensible yet adventurous.

They strive not to be poor, and they have a strong desire to eliminate the poverty of the world. They want the human race to improve in every aspect so that the planet is a better place to live. They live their own lives thinking about the golden rule: "Do unto others as you would have them do unto you."

Can You Control What You Feel?

This group of people is changing the planet for the better. Today, we are inundated with all the bad things that are happening around the world. However, world poverty has diminished greatly, despite the fact that the human race has increased significantly. In the US, the quality of life that many would consider as poor has improved significantly because more people live in homes with air conditioning, have clean drinking water, and food. They may not have a new car, but what they have is reliable. Yes, without a doubt, things have improved, but we still have a lot to do, especially to eliminate extreme poverty in other parts of the world. For that, we need people who are of the third type, with the right type of mindset.

By the way, previously, I quoted Sara Blakely, who advises to never be afraid of failing. A few years ago, I saw a news article saying that "Sara Blakely, founder of the brand Spanx, has become the first female billionaire to join the **Giving Pledge**, Bill Gates's and Warren Buffett's bid to encourage the world's richest people to give at least half their wealth to charity."

Can you imagine how fantastic it would feel if you could give millions of dollars to your favorite charities? If you could make a huge contribution to solving issues so that the lives of many, many people in the world are made significantly better? You can start wherever you are now, making a difference for others, and what you give will be returned to you tenfold.

We all have powerful and expensive cars. These cars represent our lives, our bodies, and our minds. We decide how we handle them: We can choose the speed; we can choose how well we take care of it and how we drive it. Just keep one thing in mind: **This is your life, and you will live it once.** Nobody gives you the guarantee that you will live forever. Do not be afraid to explore new things or learn something new. Do not forget to enjoy every moment of life and give value to the most important things, such as caring for your own body, caring for your mind, your own family, and other people.

Do You Give 100% in Everything?

When I make the decision to do something, I like to give 100%. This is very important for you to understand, because most people don't know what this means. If you want to be successful in your marriage, then both have to give 100%. You can't give your children only a little—no, they need 100% of you. In your business, if the people who work with you, or for you, notice that you do not deliver 100%, you will lose their respect, and they will gravitate to other people or other jobs. I'm not trying to endorse you becoming a workaholic, stressed out 100% of the time. Rather, give 100% effort to staying balanced. Focus on one thing at a time, and give that your 100% attention. Plan how you will spend your time, and practice working your plan so that you can be fully present and give 100%, no matter how short or long the time span.

It is very difficult for some people to understand how important it is to play 100% full-out every day in everything we do. Think about this for a minute. How you do anything, is how you do everything. The first time I heard that, I found it shocking. Then I started looking around at people I knew, and imagining how they would behave in alternate environments. I could see that the guy who had a messy desk at work, and left spills in the break room for others to clean up, was almost certainly a slob at home, too. I thought of a manager I knew, who was the most intense person I'd ever met. Every conversation and task was approached with serious intensity, and I imagined him then, on vacation, and I could just see him fishing with the same vigorous and concentrated effort.

Finally, I thought about the person I should have been considering—myself. Start with yourself. Does your body appear to you like it belongs to someone who gives 100% effort to taking care of it? The mirror doesn't lie; you can say what's so, and if you have any doubts, ask your giant, who never lies. If your answer is no, you should start here; if the answer is yes, I congratulate you. If you are not taking care of yourself, I guarantee that there are many areas in your life where you are not committed 100%.

About a year ago, a very successful woman was giving a speech in our Toastmasters club, and she said something that I have never forgotten. If you only commit to something 80%, you are 100% out. In other words, it is guaranteed that you will give up or quit before you achieve what you say you are committed to. (Alice Rothbauer)

So many people today are in poor physical condition. Why? They are not committed to taking care of themselves 100%. Another common issue is that marriages fail, and divorce has become more common than rare. The main reason is that one or both are not committed 100% to spending a lifetime together. They say they are "all in, forever," but they hold back on the 100% effort. You must understand something: If you want to be the kind of leader who achieves great success for themselves, and helps others, giving 100% effort is essential. If you are not committed 100%, you will not win. It's too easy for your inner monster to persuade you to give up when you hit the first speed bump or find an obstacle in your path. Since obstacles are always going to occur in life, being only partially prepared will cause you to give up and lose out. Only with a 100% mindset will you be able to respond to them and come out a winner.

The winners commit 100%. The winner knows that the mind controls the body, so let the mind of the inner giant take control. In order to deliver 100%, you need to have a clear vision and a plan, or it will be very easy to give up. It will be very difficult for you to achieve what you want by accident. That is why you must work on what you like and what you love. This is the only way you get where you want to go.

Most people are not doing what they want to do with their lives, because they are concerned about the opinions of other people. The funny thing is that other people are worried about other people's opinions too—this is a game that has no logic. Do the good things that give you great satisfaction, and give 100% of yourself. What other people think of you is none of your business.

Sometimes it is not easy to commit 100% to things; because when you deliver 100%, there is no turning back. If you have obstacles, you have to overcome them. I have a friend who tells me that in life we have to learn to build a heart from gut. Think about this for a minute. At first, this seems impossible, but often we must do what seems impossible to achieve what we want. And if we don't give up, we will achieve it. Make sure that your giant is committed to give 100% and become a great leader, and the walk of life will feel good.

Can You Control What You Feel?

Actions to take now:

What is the **one thing** that you know you must do to get out of your comfort zone or fast-laner mentality? Isolate the one next thing to do in order to let your giant guide you to have the life you most want. As long as what you want has only the potential to help yourself and others, doing no harm in any way, then feel the fear and do it anyway. Write down that **one next action**, and **by when** you will take it. Life is too short, and most people wait too long to start living it. Don't be one of those people!

Your Giant or Your Monster

Notes

Chapter 9

Are You a Leader or a Follower?

"If your actions inspire others to dream more, learn more, do more, and become more, you are a leader."
– John Quincy Adams

How Do You Know if You Are a Good Leader?

In each and every one of us, there is a potential leader. The difference between John Quincy Adams and yourself, however, may be something that is simple (but not easy) to acquire. It is the courage to let your giant take a step forward and pursue your life mission with 100% effort.

Leadership is very important for the human being. Throughout history, we can learn from men and women who have been amazing leaders. In my opinion, we are all leaders, whether we like it or not. **Because we have to lead our self**—our inner giant loves to be a leader—we have the potential to lead and "inspire others" as Adams said.

In some cases, what happens is that a person is a very bad leader because they are guided by their inner monster. Something interesting to me is that people generally like to follow other human beings—in their ideologies, beliefs, and in their actions. Millions of people have made themselves a follower of some particular person, time and time again in history. By doing this, they forget that they themselves are leaders.

You may say that a person is a good leader if he sets a good example for others, or if he has followers, or if he knows how to lead his family, a company, or a community, and so forth. All this may be true, but leadership goes even further, because **you cannot be a leader for anyone else without first being a good leader for yourself**. This is where leadership starts. You have to be a good leader for yourself before you can be an effective leader for others.

The person who manages to be a good leader of himself, wins one of the greatest battles of his life. Sadly, many people can't lead themselves. *They can't make themselves do the things they should do.* They may be super smart, popular with others, and have the best of intentions, but instead of motivating themselves to take the actions they know to take, they fly around like a kite without a tail. On the other hand, when you find a person who is a great leader, you can tell right away. They know the direction they wish to go, and they take the actions needed to stay on course. I have met many who have this excellent quality of being a self-directed leader, but often they don't even know it.

I say this from my own experience. Years ago, I started learning about leadership: What are the qualities of a good leader? Why do people follow others as their leader? What character traits do our greatest leaders have in common? Are leaders born with something others are not? How can you build your leadership skills? During my studies, I realized that I was a good leader because I could lead myself.

This realization was freeing to me, as I grasped a whole new level of understanding about who I was and who I wanted to be. I was not afraid of taking risks, I was able to motivate people to do what they needed to do, and I set a good example for my family and for others—yet I was not where I wanted to be financially, and I did not even feel like I was making much progress toward financial freedom. Knowing that I had a track record of being a good leader in some areas of life, I asked myself: What kind of leader do I have to be to improve financially?

This is what I decided to do: More planning, goal-setting, and more organization in all areas of my life. I decided to be a continuous learner, and focus on better understanding how to lead myself along the path to prosperity. I exercised my leadership strengths with those things in mind, and I started to make real progress in building wealth.

Analyze Your Leadership Effectiveness

Think about the different areas of your life, such as home and family, your church or community, and your past or current jobs. In each area, identify one time where you stepped up, where you led yourself or others to accomplish something out of the ordinary. (That is when you let your giant guide you, by the way.) Now, what qualities of leadership do you already have? What do you need to improve on to be able to accomplish more?

In my leadership studies, I noticed that most of the examples I read about were men, though I can think of many examples of outstanding women. If you are a woman, you also have to be a good leader—you must lead yourself and your family. Oh, but women don't stop here—today, millions of them are leading the world because they have excellent leadership qualities and have many followers. From professional sports teams to corporate CEOs to heads of nations, women are succeeding as leaders. Many times, I have seen women who have proven to be better leaders than many men, but what impresses me the most is seeing a woman making herself do whatever she needs to do to succeed. Today, I have more concern for young men than for women, because I notice that women are showing more persistence and more desire to get ahead than men. Maybe this is just my limited observation, but the fact is that it is never too early for both males and females to become committed to being good leaders, and we can all encourage that.

When most people talk about leadership, they talk about influence, or about all the qualities you possess, and this is great, but I like to talk about the ability that a person should have to make themselves do what they have to do. Everyone has heard that self-discipline is good, but I want you to know that it is imperative. It cannot be skipped over or worked around, and it is what you must develop in order to be successful.

Self-Directed People Can Choose to Change—and Then Follow Through

We all know people who say they want to change something about themselves, but they fail as leaders in their own lives. In the past two years, I've seen three people I know, finally decide to quit smoking. It seems that each of them did stop smoking, but I admit I was not surprised that two of them have gained a lot of weight, and the other one seems to stay half-drunk all the time. The reason why I tell you that this doesn't surprise me is because these people are not good leaders, because they have no control over themselves.

If you don't have control over yourself, you will exchange one bad habit for another bad one. It reminds me of someone who knows they need to leave the party in order to get to work on time, but instead of walking out the door, they change dance partners. For someone who quit smoking in order to improve their health, that was a hollow victory if they failed to start leading a healthy lifestyle.

If you are controlled by your inner giant, then you will be self-directed in your life, and you will be a good leader. But as I explain, it is easier to let yourself be guided by the internal monster that prefers the pleasure of the moment without thinking about the consequences of the future. Keep in mind that to become a great leader, you must take control of yourself.

Are You an Ordinary or Extraordinary Person?

When you look at very successful people, what's on your mind? Do you think that the reason they were able to succeed is because they have a special talent? Because they are gifted? Or because they were lucky? Well, in some cases this is true, but this is not true in most cases.

Lisa Nichols is a celebrated motivational speaker who has inspired millions through her seminars and her role as a featured teacher in The Secret. One thing she said, which not only impressed me but made me want to embrace and share it, is: *"You*

Your Giant or Your Monster

make me extraordinary because you want to be off the hook. We think that other people can achieve great economic success because they have some special talent or luck, and we don't." That's a big excuse, she says, and that what we have to do is pay the price, and do what we have to do to achieve what we want.

I really want you to understand this: We are all unique and special. We can show up as *extraordinary* if we make the decision and are willing to do whatever it takes to achieve what we want. It is about being constant and being a little different from people who are not very interested in improving themselves. We get to choose what kind of life we want to live, whether it is ordinary or extraordinary. Being a good leader? It is a choice, and it starts with choosing to let our inner giant be in control so that life is on course, not wasted on following trivial pursuits.

Now I have something so important to share with you, and I want you to focus ten times more than how you have been reading along thus far. I want you to do a very important exercise, one that can change your life. When you start doing this exercise, don't leave it halfway. You will need paper and pencil for this, so go ahead and get those now.

Now, to continue reading, you need to already have your writing tools handy, okay? If you think you will skip this exercise and go to the next chapter, don't do that. If you stop reading, you will never understand how valuable your existence is. Follow the steps, and experience what you feel inside—you can expect to feel/hear your inner monster as well as your inner giant.

Some time ago, I was invited to talk about my story to a group in the United States. I knew how to communicate my story, but I wanted to be able to teach them something that could significantly impact their lives in a positive way, and I didn't know what to do. Three days before my scheduled talk, I got up early, about four in the morning. What I typically do first thing in the morning is sit in the quiet and think for about 15 minutes. I had this upcoming talk in mind, and that's why I started looking inside myself for something that I could teach. I felt like my inner giant was leading me down a certain path. This is the exercise that occurred to me to do, and that I did:

I am going to give you a short phrase (five words) to think about. When I tell you to stop reading, please stop reading for 30 seconds and think or meditate on the 5 words I will be offering at the end of this preface. You will write down the first thing that came to mind. No editing; you must be honest with yourself here. Follow the exercise, and then let me give you an explanation. Are you ready? YOU AND I ARE GOD. Stop reading please, and meditate for 30 seconds. As you have thoughts, and you notice what you feel inside, write these down. Whatever judgments and opinions you have about the exercise, just keep noticing your thoughts and feelings, and writing them down AFTER you have done this exercise, and please continue reading.

Can this possibly be true, that you and I are God? Let me ask you something: When you see a person showing love for another person, without expecting anything in return, do you think you're seeing God?

I will start by telling you that God is love. If you believe that you are God, then you will strive to be the most loving person on this planet. Pride will disappear in you, and you'll have no hatred or fear, but you will feel powerful. You could have no doubt that you can be the best leader you can be. You will stop creating limits and feeling like a weak person. When you are dealing with others, you will be different because, from now on, you will begin to treat all other people as you would treat God—because they are God, just as you are.

Think for a moment if you had to deal with God every day. How would you do it? How would you behave in front of him all the time? If, today, our nature is to behave in an excellent way in front of a person we admire and respect, as perhaps in front of our parents or our boss or important client, or in front of a religious leader or the President, imagine how you will behave in front of God.

So, how do you think you would start behaving right now if you think you're God and you think that a fellow human being is God? Maybe God is inside of you, hoping that you understand that you are God, and that you make and act on a decision to change the world for the better. This is the belief of many but not of the majority.

Many explain it in a different way and teach that we are not God, but that we are the creation of him, and that we have and can demonstrate his qualities because, from him, we receive the power we need. If this is your belief, that is perfect. As long as you are demonstrating God's wonderful qualities to others, you are doing God's work, but if you are not, this belief is of no use to you. The belief that God will one day fix the problems of our planet, or let other people fix them, will not help either. When a person decides to be an excellent leader, he is always thinking about being a better person and how to help others to be better.

Every great leader wants to make a positive impact on others, though some have their family and community in mind, while others want to make a difference with millions of people and affect global change. Actually, because of the ripple effect, even the smallest courageous act as an effective leader can impact not only the small circle near to you, but others outside of your community, state, and across oceans.

The Things Great Leaders NEVER Do

I will tell you something very common today in people. When I was eighteen years old, I started in the dump truck business. One thing you can always notice about truckers is that they have a lot of time to talk. Unfortunately, there is a contagious epidemic in this business—the talk consists of 95% complaints. Most truck drivers spend all their time focused on everything negative that happens. Even if they are making money sitting under a tree waiting, without doing anything at all, they seem to have much to complain about.

The most common complaint is that they don't have money. They aren't paid enough, especially with how expensive it is to get parts if the truck breaks down or the tires need replacing. And the tires and brakes wear out too fast. And, hey, insurance costs a fortune now, and they can't afford it. Then they say that because of the President, oil is more expensive than gold. When they finish grumbling about the trucking business, they start talking bad about their wife, because she is giving them a lot of the wrong kind of food, and now they are fat and have high blood pressure. When they finish talking badly about their own wife, they start talking badly about the wife of another truck driver who happens to be thin, so they say that his wife does not cook, or that her cooking must not be fit to eat. And when that topic has run its course, then they start complaining about the weather: If it rains, this is bad because there is no work, and if it doesn't rain, there is too much dust. Like people everywhere, some complain it's too hot; at the same time, others complain it's too cold. The complaints circle around and around, along with accusations of who or what is to blame for everything. Do you think that with this kind of habit you can be a valuable leader?

Think of a great leader you have spent some time with. Are they complainers? Do they waste time complaining about things that are out of their control, or do they focus on problem-solving and constructive actions? Do they take responsibility or always point out who can be blamed? To constantly complain, blame, or shame—these are not habits of effective leaders.

I want you to ask yourself: Do I want to be mediocre, or a person who achieves greatness in everything in life? There are some pay-offs to choosing *mediocre*. You will not have to do much, and whenever you make a mistake, you can always find someone or something to blame. Choosing to be mediocre is a matter of having bad habits, such as complaining, blaming, and developing a strong sense of apathy (i.e. not really caring what does or does not get accomplished). You won't have to take big risks, and you won't have to pay huge amounts of income tax, because your income will always be mediocre.

I was convinced from an early age that I did NOT want to live a mediocre life. So, for me, to explore different opportunities and learn new things is always very important, I didn't really know which of the opportunities would give me the best outcomes, but I knew I had to search until I found the results I wanted.

Are You a Leader or a Follower?

To avoid being a mediocre person, you have to really want it. Here is where everything begins—you have to have a burning desire. Are you in touch with your deepest desires? Sometimes you realize that you once were but no longer are. Clarifying your desires is a good place to start. Most people don't reach their full potential, and arrive at old age full of regrets—then it is too late. Never wait to start accomplishing the things you want! Begin today, and then, every day, do something that brings you closer to your goals, especially if it makes you stretch out of your comfort zone.

If you lack this burning desire, start to associate with people who have that fire, and who don't give up no matter what happens. They have purpose, passion, and are clear on their life mission. They know that everything is a process and that at the end, they will succeed. Only then can you be an effective leader, with the power to leave a mark on the world. You already learned that you have access to a powerful giant that has unlimited power. You know that you are unique, that you have to believe in yourself, that you are on this planet to make it better than you found it, and that you must explore every aspect of this life that is wonderful. But I ask you, do you know why?

You are part of what exists in this universe, of the energy that surrounds us. You are part of God if you believe in him. That is why you should not feel like an insignificant person, or a person of little value. You are a precious creation. You are super special. You are part of God.

Are You Winning the Big Game?

Everything you have been reading here, so far, demonstrates that your inner monster is a loser, and your inner giant is a winner. Your monster may believe he is a winner, especially when he prevails over and over, winning the trivial games of avoiding responsibility, hiding from challenging opportunities, and keeping a tight lid on your potential for big success. Only when your giant is in control will you win the big game in life, and enjoy the freedom that success brings.

There is a big difference between the winner and a loser. *When a person is determined to win, this intentionality brings a special energy to the game.* When you are working to strengthen your giant, you must keep this in mind. Unless you are determined to win, you will never be a winner. Let me tell you something about this giant that you have inside: He is a winner. You may not know it yet, but this giant you have inside has a big heart, and that is what it takes to win.

What games do you have to win in life? Good question. The first game that a person has to win is personal: *You have to conquer yourself.* This is very simple; at the same time, it is complicated. It is simple because being able to control your own thoughts and emotions should be something that everyone can do. Now, take a minute and think about the people you know, and you will see something that might surprise you.

- Why are people overweight and not exercising?
- Why do people smoke, or use drugs or alcohol?
- Why do people spend so much time in front of television and social media?

Are You a Leader or a Follower?

- Why do people get divorced or don't have good family relationships?
- Why do people have so many economic problems?

The list could go on and on. The main reason is that they have not been able to conquer themselves. Everyone wants to be a winner, but few have personal discipline or patience—they want everything very quickly, without thinking about the consequences. Lisa Nichols said, *"...people want the convenience of transformation without inconvenience."*

In order to be able to win big in the games of life, first you have to be able to control yourself completely. You have to force yourself to do what you don't want to do, constantly, until this thing becomes your habit. Your inner giant is a winner and understands self-discipline, and he knows that if you acquire the correct habits and practice them, he can keep the momentum going. Maybe it will be difficult at first, but when you consistently practice these good new habits, they become your life. And in a short time, you will discover that the person you most admire is yourself.

Here is how one extraordinary US Navy SEAL describes this essential habit of self-control, in his book about leadership:

> *"The test is not a complex one: When the alarm goes off, do you get up out of bed, or do you lie there in comfort and fall back to sleep? If you have the discipline to get out of bed, you win—you pass the test. If you are mentally weak for that moment, and you let that weakness keep you in bed, you fail. Though it seems small, that weakness translates to more significant decisions. But if you exercise discipline, that*

Your Giant or Your Monster

translates to more substantial elements of your life."
– Jocko Willink, *Extreme Ownership: How U.S. Navy SEALs Lead and Win*

If you follow through on the small things, winning in the big game of life is much easier. But it is very difficult to be a great winner in the world if you don't win over yourself first. We can wish that it was easy, that we just naturally always wanted to do what was best for us. This is not ever the case. You cannot actually stop your monster from serving up bad ideas that are designed only to keep you comfortably mediocre—but you can empower your giant to swat them away and give them no voting power about your actions. It's a choice.

Life gets so much simpler once you choose to hand over the controls to your giant. When your giant takes control, he swats away all the bad ideas your monster constantly generates—when you (actually your monster) have the thought to eat two or three desserts, your giant will not let you. The day you don't want to go to the gym or take a walk, he will override those notions and have you tying your tennis shoes in no time. When you are tempted to pull out your credit card and waste money on something you do not need, your giant keeps your hands off your wallet. You see, there is this inner struggle going on for all of us. It may appear that some highly successful people are just breezing through life, but what you are really observing is someone whose giant is in control, fighting and winning the small and big internal battles, all day, every day.

One of the main reasons why people don't become the person they want to be is because they are too tied to, and too comfortable with, who they are in the present. *The winner is willing to let go of negative thoughts, disempowering beliefs, and bad habits, and implement different, better ones.* Each person who has become a winner has an incredible story. Why? Because to be a winner, you have to overcome difficulties, and overcoming these challenges and difficulties is what makes you stronger, and that's how you become a winner. A winner knows the truth of these words: "Man cannot discover new oceans unless he has the courage to lose sight of the shore." This quote, from Nobel Laureate André Gide, is often quoted by those looking for strength and encouragement to venture out from their safe zone.

A winner knows that there is never a lack of opportunity. A winner knows that the mind controls the body, and gives control to his giant. A winner knows that it is his responsibility to keep his physical, mental, and spiritual health as strong as possible. A winner knows that he is unique and has special qualities he can develop and leverage for his own success and to help others. A winner has a vision and a plan, and knows that those people without these will never win. A winner knows that they don't succeed by accident or pure luck. A winner has passion.

If you want to be successful, look for someone who has achieved the results you want. Who are they being? What was their course of action to get them where they are? What tools and knowledge do they have? Make a three-column list: Be/Do/Have. Do your research, and figure out how to fill in these columns about this successful person you wish to emulate. If you apply yourself, you will achieve the same result.

Are You a Determined and Persistent Person?

Who do you think is in control—your giant or your monster—when you get frustrated about a set-back, and decide to quit trying to reach your goal? Your inner monster is quick to give up, whereas your inner giant lives with the attitude: "Fall down twice, get up three times." Any set-back is met with determination to figure out a way to persevere and succeed.

Having determination is something that many people have not been able to develop. In many ways, we are born with a good amount of determination, but as we grow older and experience life's speed bumps, it can wear away and become weak. Not only is the non-stop energy level of a small child enviable, think about the persistence and determination they demonstrate as they learn to do everything for the first time. When they decide they want to walk, they literally fall down twice and get up three times. Over and over, they persevere, until they have accomplished their goal of walking, running, and chasing down the family dog. *It is essential that you reclaim this level of determination in order to become a great leader.* We have to try something over and over again, maybe changing our method, until we get the result we want.

That is why I believe that the first step to becoming a great leader is to work on oneself, to have in mind the vision of what one wants. If the internal giant is prepared, nothing can prevent us from obtaining what we want, if we use persistence and determination.

Abraham Lincoln was undoubtedly very persistent: At 21, he failed in business; at 22, he failed in the legislative race; at 24, he failed again in business; at 26, he had to overcome the death of his girlfriend; at 27, he had a nervous breakdown; he lost the election to Congress at 34, and lost the election for the Senate at 45; at 47, he was unsuccessful at becoming vice president; at 49, he lost the election to the Senate and, finally, at 52, he became the President of the United States. Who does that?! Well, you will never achieve anything close to the level of success, fame, and admiration that Lincoln did, if you don't buy into the importance of being persistent.

Life is a process that when you have the determination and persistence, in the end, you'll succeed. Sometimes you don't know how to achieve what you want, but if you are looking for opportunities and always learning something new, you will be ready when the opportunities come. This world is full of opportunities, but if we are not prepared to see them, then they will pass by. Hint: Your giant is brilliant at recognizing opportunities, so always leave him in control!

Actions to take now:

Review what you wrote during the exercise "You and I are God." Review what you wrote for the exercise analyzing a person you admire. What is your next step to model them and move yourself toward achieving similar accomplishments?

Make a commitment to your inner giant that you will play at 100%.

One of the books that you must read, or re-read, is, *The 21 Irrefutable Laws of Leadership,* by John C. Maxwell.

Are You a Leader or a Follower?

Notes

Chapter 10

What Are Your Beliefs About Money?

"Money was, is, and will be the best invention that will ever exist."
– Josue Lopez

Is Money Good or Bad?

I recently asked my son's 11-year-old friend if he hoped to have a lot of money when he grew up. His answer not only surprised me, it horrified me. "I don't want to be rich; I want to serve God."

Can you imagine if this young man goes through life believing that these are mutually exclusive paths? And making decisions with that mentality about money? He would never experience financial freedom. It is possible to serve God and have a lot of money, and there is nothing wrong, impure, or impossible about it. Since God loves us and wants the best for us, I believe God wants us all to be wealthy. The Bible does NOT say that money is the root of all evil, by the way. It says that the love of money is wrong. This relates to avarice and greed, rather than money itself.

Guy Shashaty, the Primerica Sales Director that I mentioned before, never knew how much his words changed my life: **"Money makes you more of what you already are."** I have shared them with as many people as I can, including you, so you can develop the right mentality about money. Seeking money or having money is neither good nor bad—just like any tool, money can be used for constructive or destructive purposes.

One time, Shashaty invited me to his house, a beautiful mansion, where I met his wonderful family. I knew I could learn a lot from this man because everything he said resonated with me, but I was conflicted. At the time, my giant wanted to conquer the world, but my monster still had control over me. Out of fear, I decided to pass on his offer to teach me the new business skills that were necessary. I made the excuse that I didn't think it was for me, and decided to stay in the trucking business. It is one of my biggest regrets.

Some Say Money Is Not Important

If you don't see money as something important, you will never have much. In this day and age, it is almost impossible to live without money. There are four essentials to life, and they may not be in the order you'd imagine: The first is air to breathe, because without it, we would die in minutes; the second is money, because with it, we can buy everything else we need. The third thing is water, as without it we will not live long; and the fourth and last thing would be food. Money is second on this list of four necessities, and yet some people say that money is not important. Those who think this way are controlled by their monster, which is guided by erroneous ideologies and unreasonable and limiting thoughts. Let me give you an example.

What Are Your Beliefs About Money?

Imagine that you want an apple, so you go to a marketplace where there is a vendor who has these apples that you want. Money does not exist, so you have to ask this person what you can trade in order to get one of their delicious apples. (Items of value to others are the currency used in a barter system.) He tells you that in exchange for a bag of apples, he wants a pig. You are not a farmer, so you don't have a pig, and must now go out and find someone who can provide you with one. Of course, once you find someone, you have to be able to trade something with him for his pig, and this person tells you he needs furniture. Off you go to find a carpenter, but in exchange for his furniture, the carpenter tells you he wants rice. Luckily, you have a bounty of rice to trade for the furniture, which you'll trade for the pig, which you'll trade to get that bag of ripe, juicy apples.

While this system actually worked pretty well long, long ago, it is not easily scalable. With the variety of goods and a large population like we have today, it would be extremely arduous and inefficient. Today, we can go directly to the source of what we are seeking, and use money as currency to obtain it. So yes, money is important because we all have a need of things we do not or cannot produce ourselves. Also, the more responsibilities you have, the more money you require. The less money you have, the less you are able to improve the quality of life for yourself and others.

Don't Blame Benjamin

Money is a wonderful thing that, if used responsibly, will help you live a wonderful life. The problem is that so many are controlled by their monster and—man, does he like to misuse money! Like a child with keys to a candy store, the monster has no self-control and will get you into trouble every time. Because he craves instant gratification and lacks discipline, money is just a way to support his bad habits. It's not the candy's fault that the child gorges on it and becomes sick, and the consequence of misusing money is not the fault of Benjamin (nickname for the US one-hundred-dollar bill, which bears the image of Benjamin Franklin).

Due to this misuse, millions of people have negative thoughts about money, and say that it is the "root of all evil" and that it "can't buy happiness." It is true that more than money goes into being happy, but stigmatizing it is like saying that because someone killed another person with a knife, knives are evil, violent, and cannot bring joy. (Tell that to a world-class chef!) *Neither money nor knives are to blame for what people decide to do with them. Don't blame Benjamin, but instead, figure out how he can be your best friend and partner to do good in the world.* Think of money as a leveraging tool so you can accomplish more in a shorter time frame. Your giant truly wants to do great things for the world, so you should never be ashamed to want a lot of money to help others with your life mission.

Do You Know How to Listen?

The older I get, the more I realize the importance of knowing how to listen. When I was younger, I was always working hard to get out of poverty. Little by little, I began to realize that I knew how to listen well to all the things that my parents and the people around me told me. At the time, I believed that everything they told me was logical, but as the years went by, I began to realize that that wasn't necessarily the case. I heard things like, "If you are born poor, you will always be poor," and, "You can't serve two masters; you serve God or riches." The one that always bothered me most was that "to get rich you have to step on other people." I knew that I was never going to do this, so did that mean I'd never get rich?

The first person I knew who had a lot of money, and who I thought was rich (though today I know that he was not), did not treat me very well. I worked for him and, on many occasions, felt he used his big fat thumb to crush me. All the negative things he would say to me, on a daily basis, penetrated my subconscious and put down roots. Looking back, I can see that he was wasting his prosperity on feeding his inner monster, and that monster only cared about dominating and controlling others.

Keep in mind, my family and the people around me were poor and had many unmet needs, even after we came to the United States. All we knew to do to survive and potentially improve our situation was to work very, very hard. I was glad to have any job that allowed me to earn and save a little money. When I was eighteen years old, I bought my first dump truck, the giant avocado-like piece of junk I mentioned before. Of course, it didn't have a radio, so I had a lot of time to think. I knew that there were many wealthy people in the world, but that there were many more that were poor. I was constantly asking myself, "What do I have to do to become rich?" I knew I wanted to be rich, but I had been inundated with so many negative opinions about what being rich meant, that I was conflicted.

I know now that I was listening too much to my monster inside of me, that had been raised all those years around others who were also being controlled by their monsters. All those negative things that come to mind about money are completely illogical things. In an effort to change your own negative feelings associated with money, and to teach a valuable lesson to your giant, I challenge you now to hone your listening skills and listen to those who are rich. Listen to what they think about money. Every time you choose to listen to constructive, useful advice from people who have wealth-building experience, you are feeding your inner giant. You are helping to displace the limiting beliefs of your monster, and replacing them with empowering ideas that will help you achieve wealth.

If you don't have the money you would like to have to live the life you want to live, you have to change what you know and believe. Understand that most of what you know about money is wrong and outdated. Imagine that your mind is a computer hard drive. You have to get the old, corrupt files—beliefs—out, so that you have space to begin saving new ones. Your current system is obsolete and, unless you update your program, nothing will change for you. The best way to accomplish this task is by listening.

Do You Like Change?

Let me share with you now another system that works for me as it relates to money. It is a simple and practical system that, if applied worldwide, could eliminate global poverty all together. The challenge, again, lies in its simplicity. It is so simple that most do not believe in its effectiveness and, therefore, choose not to use it. Given that your giant is already guiding you, I trust that you will begin to utilize this essential system in all areas of your life, no matter what, and will see significant improvements in no time.

What Are Your Beliefs About Money?

I like to call this system *ESS*. Each letter represents a word that I'm almost 100% sure you have used in the past—incorrectly.

Here's what most people do with their money:

EARN: They earn money.
SPEND: Then they spend it on their needs.
SAVE: If they have any money left, they save it, but most often, there is none remaining.

Doesn't this sound like the typical way people relate to money? This may seem normal, and perhaps you, too, are following this system, but it is one of the reasons why around three billion people in the world today live in poverty. Even in the U.S., where the average income is higher than most others on the planet, using this system keeps people away from ever becoming rich.

This is the system your monster knows well, and he doesn't know how to do anything else. However, your giant knows that there is a completely different and better system that works perfectly to move from poverty to wealth.

Starting today, follow this system instead:

EARN: **You earn money.**
SAVE: **You must first save at least 10% for yourself to invest.**
SPEND: **And then cover your expenses with what's left.**

"Ha! That won't work for me!" If you sense that your monster is protesting the idea of following this new system, that is normal. Remember, your monster likes to tell you things like: "It is impossible; we don't have enough money to cover our expenses," or, "What's the point of saving 10%? It will take a long time to have any significant amount saved, so why bother?" Remember that I already mentioned that this system seems so simple that most people won't even try it; for this reason, they never get out of poverty. Today, with your giant's guidance, take action. You have to pay yourself first; you earned the money, and you deserve it. This is the first step.

I first learned a version of this method from a book titled, *The Richest Man in Babylon*, by George S. Clason. I recommend that you read this book (it's small but powerful) and apply everything you will learn. It inspired me to make one simple change in habit: I began saving 10% of what I earned, and I had 90% left for all other expenses. Over time, I reduced expenses enough to start saving 20%. Little by little, I reduced expenses and increased savings more and more. When you decide to save a part of what you earn, miracles happen. If you manage to do this for a whole year, you will have instilled a habit that will serve you for a lifetime, and you will never be without money.

Once you begin saving money, the most important question becomes: What should I do with the money I am saving? Remember, *the first step is to develop the habit of saving* **(the habit of consistency)**; the *second is to invest the money you've saved so that it produces more money*. There are many different investment options available. I prefer to invest my savings into real estate by buying houses to turn into rental properties. You can also invest in a business, purchase stocks and bonds, etc. Be advised that when you start saving money, it can take some time to develop a significant amount. Use this time to learn about different investment opportunities, and which one(s) will work best for you.

Take your time and invest wisely because the last thing you want to do is lose any of the hard-earned money you have saved. *Never invest your money in something you don't understand*, just because you heard it was a good idea from someone you consider smart about money. Take time to learn about your options, ask for advice if you want, but make your own informed decisions.

Is It Really That Simple to Achieve Financial Independence?

Using this method, I was able to achieve financial independence in 14 years. Others have also used it, and their lives changed rapidly. You have heard it said that money calls money. When your conscious mind and your subconscious mind align, and your focus becomes saving the minimum 10%, other frivolous things become unimportant. Many unproductive, expensive habits start to disappear from your life, and you begin to live life on this new path. Sounds great, doesn't it? Well, I have better news yet! What if I told you that there is a more effective method that helps you achieve financial freedom even faster?

In my opinion, financial independence is one of the most important goals that all people should attain. Why? Well, let me first explain what financial freedom or financial independence means for me. Financial freedom, in my opinion, is when a person lives where they want to live, in a house they love, with the comforts they want. These comforts may include nice cars or a boat and so on. Now, did you notice that my definition of financial freedom did not include living in an oversized house and owning a yacht or helicopter? *My philosophy is that when a person feels comfortable with their lifestyle, and can maintain that lifestyle without having to work, they are financially independent and free.*

For a person to achieve this level of freedom, he or she must not be solely focused on earning an income, saving, and spending wisely—they must not only work for money but have money working for them. I'm talking about having passive income.

Everyone needs money to live, of course. You need a source of funds that will produce enough money every month to maintain your lifestyle. For example, if you need $4,000 every month to maintain your lifestyle comfortably, your income source has to produce at least $4,000 a month. The source of that income can be from rental properties you own or your business income, etc., but it must be at least $4,000—preferably a little more so that you can have extra money to invest. Once you have reached the level of incoming money flow that you need to, you will be financially free. Becoming financially wealthy is another level all on its own.

The day you have the time and passive income to support your desirable lifestyle, you will be considered a free man or woman. If you have to go to work every day because you have to pay all your expenses and feed your family, you are not yet financially free. Imagine the day when you no longer have to worry about money, when you can wake up and say, "What do I want to do today?" What are the things that you would do if you didn't have to worry about making sure enough income was coming in to pay your bills and feed yourself and your family? How clear is your plan to achieve this state of living?

What Are Your Beliefs About Money?

Your giant must have a clear picture of what financial freedom means to you, because if it is not clear, it will be harder for him to be your partner. You and your giant must be aligned, and understand why you are doing things a certain way—why you are making certain sacrifices. Keep the big, clear picture in mind, and believe in it.

Imagine when you achieve your own financial freedom. Many people say that if they didn't have to, they'd never work again. If this describes you, I believe you feel that way because you hate what you do for a living. The truth is, however, that humans generally like to be busy and feel productive. We like to create, we thrive when we grow, and that growth makes us feel happy. Having a J.O.B...not so much.

Think about what you would do if you had 100% control over the type of work you engaged in each day. In my case, I enjoy buying cheap, ugly, and neglected houses and fixing them up. Doing many of the renovation projects myself keeps me entertained and challenged. I think about how I want it to look at the end, I like to leave the property in good condition so that other people can live comfortably in it. Maybe you still call this "work," and truthfully, it is, but sitting in front of the television all day every day is no life for me.

If you like to paint landscapes, imagine doing this and then selling them. If you like fashion, imagine designing your own clothing line. If you like to fish, you could make some money dedicating your time to taking people out for fishing excursions. Perhaps you would like to sit down and write that book you've always dreamed of writing. When people say, "With enough money, I'll never want to work again," I think what they really mean is that they don't want to continue working in a job that brings them no joy or satisfaction, and I can't blame them for that one bit.

The Learning Habit

The first step to achieving financial independence is to become a good investor. How? Well, you are doing it right now by dedicating your valuable time to read this book. You have to invest in yourself more than in anything else. After all, you are the best investment opportunity that you will ever have. Unfortunately, most people are too busy scrolling social media and watching television, so they have little time left to invest in themselves in valuable ways. If you want to be healthy and in good physical shape, you have to take time to learn about that. If you want to have peace and happiness, you have to take time to learn about that. If you want to achieve financial freedom and have more free time and money, you have to take time to learn about that, too. It's that simple. In today's world, the terrific thing is that anything you want to learn about is right at your fingertips.

The key question is: What should you learn about? Nowadays, people are experts in many things, but that doesn't automatically guarantee them a better quality of life. Learning something new is always important, but in our world, which is overflowing with information, you can spend years reading, day in and day out, and yet not learn anything useful that will help you improve your life. If your goal is to have enough money to not have to worry about it anymore, then devote yourself to studying the laws of money that exist, in order to earn and save that money.

What Are Your Beliefs About Money?

What's important to understand is that the amount of money you have directly correlates to the amount of knowledge you have about money. Let me explain: I have friends who claim to be experts on money, but they have very little of it. Every time the subject of money comes up, they have endless excuses for why they do not have enough. I will tell you clearly: If you don't have enough money, it is because your head is full of incorrect beliefs and information (you have the wrong programs), and what you know does not and will not work.

When you're speaking with a person who has more money than you, don't say anything; just listen and learn. You have to empty the garbage in your mind, and make room to learn the principles and laws that other successful people have discovered and used.

Multi-millionaire and businessman, T. Harv Eker, says in his book, *The Secrets of the Millionaire Mind*, that most people have problems with their "money tree." The fruits they are producing are bad because the roots have problems. The roots are the beliefs within your mind. If you fix the roots, without a doubt you will produce a tasty and juicy fruit.

To become a new person, with a different mentality, and improve your life in a short period of time, it is vital that you develop the habit of constantly learning valuable information. Remember, one of the keys to life is to be better today than you were yesterday, in every way, and to achieve this, you have to be a constant learner.

I believe that everything you need to know to create the life you want is already in your DNA. In other words, you have it inside you. You have within your DNA the necessary power, the necessary wisdom, and the desire, but you have to find different ways to uncover and activate these things. The best ways to do this are by reading self-help books, watching videos on YouTube that inspire you, attending different seminars, or finding a coach or mentor to guide you so you can discover your full potential. Your job is to put information in, so you can discover what is inside and bring it out.

From Whom Do You Need to Learn, in Order to Have Money?

We humans tend to have preconceptions in our minds, and when those notions are challenged, meaning that we hear something different, we quickly begin to draw our own conclusions, or instantly reject anything else that may be suggested, because it doesn't make sense to us. It's not a match for what we already *know*. Recognize that this attitude is the attitude of your inner monster and is an attitude that will hold you back. Once you understand this, you'll freely let yourself be guided by your inner giant, who is humble and always likes to learn how to create a more meaningful life.

When your giant hears something that at first does not seem logical, he keeps an open mind in order to capture all of the information being shared. Then he asks: From whom does this information come? Your giant can comprehend that if the person who is speaking has a lot of money and wealth-building experience, and has achieved financial success, then he or she is worth listening to, and their advice is worth heeding. The simple fact is that learning how to have more of your own money is easier if you learn from people who already have it.

What Are Your Beliefs About Money?

The people I know who are always complaining about not having enough money (and looking for someone to blame), fail to accept that they do not have money, *because their mentality about money is all wrong.* Up to this point, what you know and how you think about money, has given you what you have. If you don't like what you have, then you can immediately see that you have to learn more about money, and think differently about it. I don't know if you've noticed that I have not even mentioned earning more. That's because before making more, you need to learn how to manage it well (including using ESS in the right order).

Making money is the easy part—keeping the money that you earn can be the hard part, especially if you don't have the wisdom and right tools to help you. I already explained that you must save at least 10% of the money you earn, and that you have to save this money before spending money on anything. But what if you divide everything you earn, in different percentages?

For example:

- The first 10% to become financially free;
- another 10% for your own education (remember, always be learning);
- another 10% to have fun every week, or once a month, with your family or friends;
- and, lastly, 70% for your other expenses, such as bills, groceries, and gas.

Recently, I was speaking at a high school, and the teacher said to me: "You have to keep 10% to give to God." The truth is that you decide how to manage and disperse your money. With that said, it is wise to be generous and charitable as much as makes sense in your own situation. This is part of having a mentality of abundance, and knowing that the more money you receive, the more you can help others. This is like welcoming money to flow into your life from wherever it is now, because with your giant in control, it will be used wisely.

Actions to take now:

Set up a simple system to manage your money, including the practice of setting at least 10% aside in SAVINGS, first. Think through the best way for you to stay on top of your money management. For example, I have six different bank accounts, and I know exactly what percentage goes into each one.

If you need additional help, you can go to www.buildingyourgiant.com/bonuses to get exclusive access to additional content and watch a free bonus video on how money works. The books that you must read are *Secrets of the Millionaire Mind,* by T. Harv Eker and *The Millionaire Booklet*, by Grant Cardone.

Your Giant or Your Monster

Notes

Chapter 11

Accepting the Gift

"You are always special; nothing can change that."
– **Elizabeth Smart**

What Should You Do Now?

You can read this book and contemplate some new ideas, and perhaps even tell others about it (yes, please!), but you and I both know, that is quite different than absorbing all the lessons and truly learning them through application in your life.

You may feel overwhelmed by the number of suggested changes you need to implement in order to see the fruits of your labor. I don't want you to feel that way. It may seem like too much at the beginning, but you will see that in a short period of time, it becomes simple. I do not know where you are in your life right now—maybe you have to make many changes, or maybe just a few. No matter the case, don't live up to what I mentioned previously about humans complicating simple things.

Imagine that you just received a gift from me; you can choose to live anywhere in the world. Picture the most beautiful and idyllic location that you can dream of. Maybe it's on the side of a mountain, facing the aqua blue sea, or maybe it's at the top of a skyscraper in New York City, with a bird's eye view of Central Park. This perfect place that you have imagined is all yours. I will buy it and give it to you. This place represents your life. Your life was given to you, and just being alive is magnificent—all the good that you can imagine is within you and around you.

Now that you are in the location of your dreams, imagine you are standing outside, smiling and gazing at your ideal home. Whether it's an enormous mansion or a quaint little cottage, the exterior is perfect. But what about the interior? What if you looked in through a window and saw that everything was a disaster? What would you do if all you saw was broken furniture, floors littered with trash, and no hint of beauty or order? The outside is idyllic, but the inside is a mess! Obviously, you must clean and organize what is on the inside before you could dwell in your perfect house in your perfect location. *The inside of your dream residence represents what is inside your own mind, body, and spirit.* Only you know the true condition of your inner self.

Maybe you have thought about what you've been reading here, and you realize that your interior is in good shape and that you only need some minor paint touch-ups and reorganizing. Or, maybe it's full of garbage and needs a deep, thorough cleaning. Perhaps when you look inside, you realize that you need a complete renovation. What are you going to do right now to get your living space in order? Remember, **you were given an amazing gift**—your inner world includes a mind, all the workings of a physical body, and a spirit. These make up your only living space.

Are you going to keep tolerating the clutter, the broken areas, and the clouds of dust? Or are you going to take action and start the cleaning and remodeling process? If you are still reading this book, I am sure you are ready to improve your life, and by now you have made the decision to let your inner giant take control. That's why it is vital that you remember to start with one thing at a time. You can't clean and renovate the new home all at once; first, you need the tools to do the work. The same goes for your life, and for that, the first thing you need is a pencil and a notebook.

Remember, your giant and your monster are always competing, and sometimes it can feel like they are at war. Like any big battle, in order to successfully accomplish the task at hand, you have to have a clear plan of attack. Determine and write down what needs to be done first to prepare you for the bigger, more challenging feats later. Remember, your monster will try to discourage you from the progress you are making, because he wants everything to stay as it is. Mediocrity can feel safe and comfortable, at least for the short term.

Don't Settle for Less Than Excellence

Keep your giant at the forefront of your mind and your actions, and make sure he outplays the monster as you work little by little in all the different areas of your life. Tackling one thing at a time, but always moving forward and enjoying the process, your ideal life, both inside and out, will soon show itself.

One of the most helpful exercises you can do is to make a list of everything you have been putting up with. Whether it is in your physical space, at home, at work, or in your relationships or

Your Giant or Your Monster

personal health—in any area of your life, you can identify and eliminate all the negativity that has clouded your life and consumed your energy, one at a time. List chronic annoyances, even ones that seem very small, such as a button missing off your favorite shirt. Some challenges are much bigger, but if they are identified and tackled, they can get resolved, usually faster and more easily than you may imagine.

Oh, does your monster hate this process! Becoming a person of excellence means you are moving out of mediocrity, clearing out negative issues, and energizing your highest intentions. Once you have your list, set about handling one at a time.

What if you have a large, looming, long-term bad habit that you feel helpless to resolve? We have all heard the analogy that "how you eat an elephant" is "one bite at a time." The key to resolving a bigger challenge is to break it down into small steps. Write it down, and then ask yourself, "What is the one next action I need to take toward eliminating this?" If you then write down something that still feels rather large and difficult, you didn't come up with a small enough step yet, so ask again until you know you've identified the one thing you can and will do, now. Then find the next one action to take, and do that. Use your self-discipline and perseverance to keep at it until you've crossed it off your list.

A side benefit is that this new awareness process empowers you to stop adding to the list! You will automatically become much more responsive, handling things quickly and effectively, before they become enlarged annoyances or difficult problems. This is one of your giant's favorite tasks, so give him the green light to become an excellence zone only. This is one of the greatest gifts

Accepting the Gift

you can give yourself and your giant.

You Are Special

I graduated from the *University of Hard Work*. I got a bachelor's degree in breaking my back, but not in making money, and I learned that working hard is not enough to improve your economic standing. I heard someone say that you needed to "work smart" rather than only "work hard." That sure sounded good, but how? Eventually, I realized that I had no choice but to try something different. I needed to learn how to work smart, so I decided to work on myself, on my giant. I was very shy, I had low self-esteem, and I did not speak English well, let alone read it. The one thing I did have going for me, though, was a burning desire to succeed, and this made the difference. Many people do not have it, but if you do, you have something very valuable. Whether or not you use this desire to spur you to action and success is your own choice.

Take time to reflect on the masses. Are most people living lives of prosperity, health, and happiness? Sadly, no. Whatever you see the majority of people doing, do the opposite. Most people are only looking for the easy way, and are waiting for the train of luck that rarely comes. *Remember, never on this planet existed before, or will ever exist, someone like you*. You are already different, but to achieve your dreams, you must also be special.

On a scale of one to ten, what level of success do you want to reach in your life? I do not mean only financially but in every area of your life—spiritually, mentally, physically etc. I imagine that you, and everyone else in the world, would not claim to be satisfied at a level four or five; we all would like to reach our maximum potential. I emphasize those words, *would like*, because *if you really want a level ten lifestyle, you have to become a level ten person.* This cannot be achieved by being average, hoping for a miracle, or wasting time with pointless things. That is where most people give up on the maximum possible, and settle for less. They literally choose to tolerate a level of being poor, unhealthy, and unhappy—some have a greater capacity for tolerance than others.

If you feel that you are already living a level eight lifestyle, and you are happy and want for nothing, then I sincerely respect that. But if you have a burning desire to reach higher levels, then I assure you that you can, and you will, as long as you do the necessary work on yourself. You see, a person operating at a level six produces a level six life. A person operating at a level ten will produce a life to match. The more you work on yourself, the higher level at which you operate, the easier it will be to reach the level of life you want. Again, this goes beyond just being different; you must be special.

Do not get me wrong; everyone chooses the life they want to live, and this must be respected. It is wise to let every person practice their own free will. Your job is not to be their judge and jury. When I tell you to be special, I'm not suggesting that you treat others as if you are better. Keep in mind that the poor-minded person creates a poor life, the mediocre person creates a mediocre life, the extraordinary person creates an extraordinary life, and, in my opinion, if you can create an extraordinary life for yourself, your family, and for other people, why wouldn't you?

For your life to improve greatly, there is a hard truth that you must accept: *Everything that happens to you is perfectly aligned*

Accepting the Gift

with who you are. Pause and meditate on these words. It is common to feel confused, or offended, or even angry. If that's the case, then your inner monster still holds a place of power in your life. He always feels like a victim of others or things that go wrong. He does not know what personal responsibility is, and is always looking for someone else to blame. Your giant, on the other hand, understands that only you are truly in control of who you are, and that in order to grow in every way, personal responsibility must be a way of life.

Let me be more specific: If you do not have enough money to feel financially secure, whose fault is it? Maybe you blame your wife, who spends every single penny you make. Or, maybe your husband does not do well in business, and spends more than he earns. Well, you are the person who allows it to continue. You may say: My children have made very bad decisions, and they have caused me a lot of trouble. Were you not the one who raised them? If they have grown to adult age, why are you allowing their life decisions to direct your life? Or maybe you say: I don't have peace, happiness, discipline, or self-control. I'm not persistent, I lack value, and I don't have enough education.

Maybe you have many stories, explanations, reasons, or excuses to be or feel that way. All that will change when you point the finger at yourself and recognize and accept that everything is your choice, no one else's. Once you finally do that, you can ask yourself: "If everything is my choice, then that means I'm responsible for navigation…what am I going to do to correct my course?" From that day on, your life will follow another direction, which will lead you to the life you dream of. From that day on, you will understand what it is to be a different, special person.

You, Without Limits

If your daily life has become a routine, this means that you are not working on developing yourself every day. Therefore, you are not growing and gaining the qualities needed to reach the next level in your life. Falling into a daily routine is like time standing still—you are not going forward or backward; you're just surviving. Work, eat, and sleep, and tomorrow you repeat. We fall into these ruts and begin to feel comfortable because we resign ourselves to accept misery as the norm. We get a lot of agreement from others that "Mondays are horrible," and that our job is just "the daily grind." Little by little, we begin to feel a void, and we do not even know why. The reality is that we, as humans, need to feel that we are growing, that we are moving forward, to feel a true sense of satisfaction and happiness. That's why our growth has to be constant.

It really is a unique and strong human craving. A dog may enjoy learning a new trick if you give him lots of treats, petting, and reinforcement. But if it has been three months, and you have not taught him one single new thing, he is just as happy! He does not feel resigned, depressed, or apathetic. Don't underestimate your inherent desire to learn, grow, and evolve. Your giant within has a voracious appetite for learning.

In order to ensure consistent growth, you must understand that all things of value require an uphill climb or a swim against the current. **No pain, no gain**.

"The game has its ups and downs, but you can never lose focus of your individual goals, and you can't let yourself be beat because of lack of effort." – Michael Jordan.

Accepting the Gift

Let me give you another example: Imagine that our planet is made up of small islands. You learn as a child that when you reach a certain age, you are required to leave your home island and swim to another island as a rite of passage. There, you will settle and start a family of your own. From an early age, you are introduced to the waters that surround your home island; first by just stepping in up to your ankles, and then by learning to float on the surface. As you get older, you continue to practice and strengthen your swimming skills until you are an expert. Then the time comes for you to find your own island. Even though you've never seen it, you fully believe that it exists, and you will find it if you trust yourself, take the risk, and never give up. Even if you feel a little afraid, there is no hesitation to set out on your important quest when it is time to do so.

I admit that this is a metaphor that probably came into my mind because of my own background of being born in the island nation of Cuba. I like to compare this scenario to that of your childhood or your youth. Until you reach a certain age or graduate high school or college, you may reside on the comfortable island where your parents or family have settled. When the time comes for you to build your own life—to find your own island—you have to believe that the success you seek is out there, and with hard work, some risk, and perseverance, you will find it. The only other alternative is to resign yourself to living your life on your home island, where you can try to get your parents or other people you already know to take care of you.

If you are a young reader, I will tell you that most do not spend enough time preparing to go out in search of their own island. Playing video games, scrolling through social media, or binge-watching shows does not strengthen the skills and mentality required to embark on a quest to build a great life. But you are not typical. Simply by reading this book, I can tell that you are ready to find your own island, or to improve the one you've already found. As for others, when the time comes to face the realities of life, they will have trouble staying afloat, and will oftentimes find themselves drowning in things like stress, depression, and debt.

For my readers who are getting up in age but are not satisfied with how they are doing in life, it's time to brush up on your swimming skills and prepare for the swim of a lifetime. By reading this book, that's exactly what you've been doing, and you should be proud. No matter our age, when we become adults, we have to decide to create our own lives. Sometimes we jump into the water on our own; sometimes our parents have to push us. Sometimes we swim against the current, and sometimes it flows in our favor. Nonetheless, if we don't get in the water, and we are not willing to lose sight of the shore for a time, we will never have the chance to live an amazing life.

Imagine now that after swimming for a while, you finally reach the shore of a new island. Exhausted from your efforts, you are happy to be on land, but your excitement is short-lived. As you explore the island, you realize that there is not enough water, very little shade, and no shelter in which to live comfortably. Many in this predicament would give up on their dreams of finding the ideal island, all the while complaining and blaming others for their bad luck. You, however, remember that you have a powerful and intelligent inner giant, full of wisdom, and you begin to wonder: What if I went in search of a better island? What can I use to get there quicker?

Accepting the Gift

You find enough resources to allow you to eat, drink, and work on your plan. With a lot of hard work, you build a small but sturdy raft; but you are now faced with leaving behind everything you've come to know, in order to leave and search for something that may or may not exist. After all, you happened upon one disappointing island, and who is to say that you won't end up somewhere just as bad or worse?

Wanting more for your life, you face your fears and go out into the unknown in search of something you can't see. *It takes faith and courage.* Many never make that decision, and stay stuck in the same place for their entire lives, but not you.

> *"A small body of determined spirits, fired by an unquenchable faith in their mission, can alter the course of history."*
> – Mahatma Gandhi

When you make the decision to leave, you start out fervently rowing your raft, excited about what awaits. Eventually, you get tired, grow hungry and thirsty, and get caught up in bad weather. At times, you question your decision to leave the old island, but because you are persistent and have a burning desire to succeed, you never stop rowing. Finally, you arrive at another island and feel the joy of succeeding after a struggle. Not only that, this island offers what you were seeking: There are fresh water springs, many opportunities for hunting food, and there are people—friendly people. Here, you fall in love and start a family.

Over time, though, the island becomes overpopulated, there is a drought, and the quality of life is diminished; you are working hard just to barely survive. Most of the island people sit around and complain but do nothing to remedy the situation. You do not waste your time and energy on complaining, but instead, you enlist your family to help you build a boat with a design that is sure to carry you and your family quickly to another, more desirable island.

People who are guided by their internal giant never stop thinking about improving their lives and the lives of others. They are always working on themselves and continually looking for new islands or new opportunities in life, while keeping in mind that the adventure of sailing and discovery is as important as the success they seek. Motivated by the new things they learn and experience, they begin to feel that they have no limits. So, how do you feel?

The Importance of Being Refined

When you hear the word, *refined*, what comes to mind? Maybe you envision refining oil or refining gold. Perhaps you imagine a refined British lady drinking her afternoon tea. Maybe you have not used this term to refer to yourself before, but I want you to go for becoming refined, anyway. First, we have to understand what this word means. Essentially, refining is a process where impurities or unwanted elements of a substance or thing are removed, perhaps part of an industrial process. It can also refer to improving something by making some changes to fine-tune it or make it more precise.

Every single day, the use of refined oil is part of life. Do you know anything about this process? The oil is taken from the earth in a state that is known as crude oil. In this state, it has very little utility. For this oil to become something useful, it has to be refined. The refining process is done inside a distillation tower,

Accepting the Gift

with crude oil deposited and heated at an extremely high temperature. The oil begins to evaporate, and different gases start to rise. Within the tower, there are different tanks designed to hold these different gases, which will be used for different purposes: Every 159 liters of crude oil will produce about 73 liters of gasoline, 35 liters of diesel, 20 liters of airplane fuel, 6 liters of propane, and 34 liters of various fuels. I am not an expert in this oil refining process, nor do I intend for you to be, but I want you to understand that for oil to be useful to people, it needs to be refined.

People are no different. We too need to go through a refining process in order to be useful in this world. The more refined we are, the better life we can live, and the more we can contribute to the well-being of others and to our planet. You came to this planet in a raw state. When you were born, nobody knew exactly what you would become, only that you were different from anyone else in this world. *You have fingerprints that belong only to you, and you have an inner light that shines only as yours can. I believe your inner giant is what shines within you, creating a burning desire for an abundance of all good things.*

As we grow up, we all go through a state of refinement. The refining process is different for everyone since we all have different personalities, intelligence levels, ethnic backgrounds, and nationalities. We live different experiences, beliefs, and cultures, and we have been raised in different circumstances. All these things that we experience can defeat us or strengthen us and make us better.

I've heard people speak of the U.S. Navy SEALS as being some of the toughest, most capable and determined people on earth. A

SEAL once told me, "From great adversity comes great strength. Just as the hardest steel is forged in the hottest fires, so too, we humans are forged and strengthened through our own struggles and triumphs."

In the process of refinement, oil must be heated to extreme temperatures. When we are feeling the intense heat of life's challenges, we are being *forged by fire*, and we are in the process of becoming highly refined, a person of value. When life does not seem to be going well, choose to persevere, because nothing starts out perfect, and everything in life goes through a process of refinement.

When we have become our best and strongest, we can change the lives of millions in this world. By accepting the gifts of our giant, we become a gift for many other people.

Mission, Vision, Purpose, and Goals

In Chapter 3, we talked a little about life mission, vision, purpose, and goals. These are all of great interest to your inner giant. The vast majority of successful people I've met always talk about these things, but to my surprise, the opinions of these people can be quite different. Some say that you have to have a life purpose, and others say that you should have a life mission. Others say that you should have a vision, which is the vehicle that you use to fulfill your mission or purpose, and others think that vision is the ability to think or plan the future with imagination or wisdom. When it comes to goals, some say that goals are what you do step-by-step to achieve what you want, and others say that the goals are what you will accomplish at the end. Some people say that you have to have goals, and others advise against it, instead

Accepting the Gift

encouraging the use of a system to do everything one step at a time. My opinion of these various opinions is that everyone is right; they are different interpretations with the same objectives.

My wife and I decided to become members of Quantum Leap, a program of Success Resources of America. Because of this, we have been able to participate in different courses, where the coaches always begin by saying: "Do not believe a word I say." That gets your attention, right? Actually, it is a great reminder that we should do our own research, thinking, and analysis, instead of simply tuning in to what some *expert* is saying, and *believing* it without serious consideration. Everything they teach comes from their own experiences, and because we all have different experiences and different ways of seeing things, the best thing you can do is simply listen to everything the person has to say. If what they say makes sense to you, great; but if it does not, draw your own conclusions. There's nothing wrong with doing this, as long as your conclusion give you the result that you desire and it influences the lives of others in a positive way.

I will share with you my own philosophy. First, my life mission:

"My mission is to eliminate poverty from people's minds and their lives."

Now I would like to ask you, what is your life mission? In other words: What do you want to do in your life time to impact the world in a positive way? You must take some time to think about what your life mission will be. Think about the things you have experienced in your life that you do not want others to endure. What extraordinary challenges have you found ways to overcome? From these experiences, as well as what you find yourself most interested in, you can discover your life mission. This is one of the things I will help you discover in my workshop.

If you are still not sure what to write, write something that you believe would change the world for the better if it could be achieved. The process of writing something is extremely important. You may not have all the details, or you may not be sure, but you have to start somewhere. If you haven't figured out your life mission yet, you must watch the bonus video on mission, go to www.buildingyourgiant.com/bonuses, and request your access to the additional material on the site.

Maybe at this moment you don't see the point of having a life mission. You just want to live a good life with your family, and let everybody else fix their own problems or challenges. Your opinion must be respected, but I urge you to keep in mind that the inner monster's way of thinking is very small, and usually does not create a life of satisfaction, joy, and abundance. That is why, when you think this way, you create limits. Having a life mission makes you see life in a different way, and it forces you to grow more each day, and when you grow, this gives you lasting satisfaction. When you have a purpose, you will get up every day with a desire to do something to be able to fulfill it. This is how you empower your giant and weaken your monster.

For example, my wife and I made financial freedom one of our biggest priorities, we wanted to come out of poverty first, so we worked hard week by week, month by month, and year by year to accomplish that goal, to fulfill our purpose. In all those years, we were always helping the rest of the family get out of poverty. After achieving financial freedom, we have been able to help in a more meaningful way. This is how I carry out my life mission.

Accepting the Gift

Perhaps you want to pay off all of your bad debt. What you do daily, weekly, monthly, or yearly are your goals to fulfill your purpose, and your vision is the vehicle or medium you are using to achieve it all. In my case, it was my trucking business and investing in houses to rent. For you, perhaps the vision is your career or profession, or your own business. When you manage to get out of debt, you may be able to establish a company to help others avoid getting into debt themselves, or help those that are already in debt to get out of it faster. In this case, your life mission may be: To help others make better financial decisions in order to live a better quality of life. What I want you to keep in mind is that your giant needs to be very clear about your life mission, vision, purpose, and goals, in order to move in the right direction. Clarity is key, as I will discuss later in this chapter.

What You Should Do Now

I want to congratulate you for having the discipline and making the commitment to read this book. Today, you should know that you are special, and you are on your way to becoming extraordinary. At the beginning of 2019, I was talking to a friend who was working hard to improve his life, and I shared with him that he was an abnormal person. You can imagine his reaction, as most people generally don't like to be described as such. While some may get offended at being called "abnormal," I consider it a compliment. In fact, I want to be abnormal because, to me, being normal means never leaving your comfort zone and doing the same thing as everyone else, most likely under the control of your monster. However, those that are controlled by their inner giant are considered abnormal because they behave differently from the rest, and that's the kind of life I want to live..

Your Giant or Your Monster

In this book, you have learned many valuable lessons that will help you to better understand yourself. Now is the time to put them into practice to live the life you want. You now know that what you believe, think, say, and do is because your giant—or your monster—controls you. If the things you say are in accordance with your life mission and your purposes, and inspire you so that you can live the life you want to live, and you can help others, then you know that your inner giant is guiding you. If it is not, you know that you are being controlled by your monster, and you have to domesticate it so that it does not control your life.

Here you are, ready to zoom ahead on your path to wealth and all the success you want in your life. But in the past, you may have also felt ready, and yet you never achieved the outcome you wanted. You may have felt a high level of motivation from something you heard or read, or realized in a big "Ah-ha!" moment in life, but the drive soon stalled out.

There are several typical causes of a financial independence plan getting weaker, stalling out, and being abandoned by the side of the road to success. One reason I want to emphasize is based on this: VELOCITY IS A FUNCTION OF CLARITY. The points covered again and again in this book have been about you getting more and more clear on what you want and why you want it. For example, if you do not yet have a written life mission that strongly resonates with you, then you need to do more work until you have clarity. Since velocity is a function of clarity, the more you crystallize your thinking and connect with your heart about your life mission, the faster you will progress toward accomplishing it.

Accepting the Gift

You may be hearing your monster and your giant each having something to say about this right now. Your monster prefers to keep things vague, as it helps him avoid being held accountable. Your giant seeks clarity and longs to understand his life mission, but may struggle with knowing when he has enough certainty and confidence. Your monster is a master of distraction, and constantly gives you options to pursue. Some people spend all of life chasing after tempting ideas (especially *get-rich-quick* schemes). They say, how can I know if it is a great idea unless I explore it or try it out? This is a favorite trick of your monster because there are an infinite number of possible pursuits that have nothing to do with what you really want in your life. You cannot live long enough to try everything, and there is no need to. What you must do, instead, is get more and more clear on what you want, so that you can easily and quickly recognize a perfectly-fitting opportunity for you when you see it. This is illustrated beautifully in the following story I heard from a banker.

As part of the extensive training to work in a bank, he had to learn all about counterfeit money. People with a fake $100 bill often ask a bank to give them (10) ten-dollar bills in exchange as a way of swapping bad money for good. Of course, all denominations, and even coins, are circulated as counterfeits. He shared that during training he was overwhelmed at the thought of having to scrutinize all the examples the trainer passed around the class. He was relieved but perplexed when the trainer told the class they did not need to study the fake money at all. He wondered, if a banker could not spot a counterfeit, who could? He was asking the wrong question.

The trainer spent the entire class time teaching about the REAL money: all the US currency denominations, old and new, and coins, which were authentic and not counterfeit. He had to learn how to hold a bill up to the light, and what to look for. He learned about the holograms that should be there and how a thin vertical strip is revealed, containing the text that spells out the bill's denomination. He learned how to look for the micro-printing and watermarks that should be in precise places on a bill. Real money had a certain weight and feel to the paper. He learned how to tilt a bill in the light to see if a certain numeral shifted from green to black. These were all the characteristics of the real thing. These, he must know, with full understanding and confidence.

Once the bankers knew with certainty what money was supposed to look like, they could simply focus on that knowledge. No matter what counterfeit versions crossed their counter, if it was different from the real thing, they knew to treat it as counterfeit, not as good money. By knowing what was real, imposters showed up for what they were, right away.

By knowing your giant, and having clarity on your life mission, purpose and goals you can easily identify and dismiss all those counterfeit ideas that your monster is always trying to pass off as real. Investing the time now to gain clarity will save you an enormous amount of time in the future.

This Is Not a Dress Rehearsal for Life

You deserve all the good that this world can offer, and you are here to explore every aspect of your life, but keep in mind that you will not live forever. Have a sense of urgency to take action and fulfill your goals step by step. Use the D.K.A.R. formula

Accepting the Gift

(Discipline, Knowledge, Action, Results) as covered in Chapter 5. Always keep in mind the tools that you possess in your mind, for they are all you need to become the type of person you admire. We come into this world like a diamond in a rough state. What gives the true value to the diamond is how it's cut, refined, and polished. As the years go by, and we grow and get older, the things that we go through leave marks on our soul. These marks can either diminish our value or they can add to our beauty and uniqueness.

Think of that internal giant that you have, and imagine it being completely balanced. Imagine yourself having total control over your emotions and feelings. See yourself with no limits, capable of achieving everything you set out to achieve, and making a difference in the lives of others. You can do wonderful things in this world, and explore every aspect of this life, if you don't set limits.

Envision yourself completely free in every way. The best place to start is financially. If you work hard to achieve financial freedom, everything else will fall into place. Your lifestyle will improve, as will your ability to contribute to improving the lives of others.

The best time is NOW, so DO IT. Right NOW. With your giant on your side, you will create the life you want and deserve to live.

Actions to take now:

Every day, make a habit of writing down three good ideas that you can implement to improve your present life, to make it more abundant in joy and wealth. Write about improving your financial situation, your body, your family, your business, etc. This habit will create connections in your mind, which will create even more ideas.

Lastly, review the **Actions to take now** at the end of every previous chapter, and bring your 100% effort to engaging with these and completing them—just to show your monster who is boss—that is, your GIANT. Make sure that you visit www.buildingyourgiant.com for additional information, products and services and also www.buildingyourgiant.com/bonuses to get access to the additional bonus materials.

Accepting the Gift

Notes

About the Author

Josue Lopez Daniel was born with a generous heart but surrounded by poverty. His experience as a child growing up poor in rural Cuba was the biggest motivator in his decision to find a way to achieve wealth and financial freedom. Fate brought him to the US at age 12, and at 16, he started his first business, continued working hard in different ventures, and became financially free by age 38.

Lopez soon found that people he knew, and also those he started meeting, were intrigued by his story, his unique path to financial independence. He made the decision to become a motivational speaker and trainer. Today, he is on a mission to eliminate poverty from people's minds and lives. He is helping people become extraordinary human beings so that no matter what happens in their lives, they can always find the strength to create success and live their dreams.

Known for his entrepreneurial spirit and people-centered leadership style, in between speaking engagements, Lopez runs several companies. His constant focus is on personal growth and learning, and he is a recent graduate of T. Harv Eker's signature program, "Quantum Leap with Success Resources." Besides reading inspiring nonfiction, and writing his own books, he participates in high-value experiences, including membership in Toastmasters International.

With his wife, Keren, and son, Josue, Jr., he resides in Bradenton, Florida. For fun, he likes fishing, diving, and traveling around the country with his family. Meeting new, successful people, and learning from their experiences, is what inspires him and fuels his passion for helping others.

To Contact Josue
(941)243-2306
www.buildingyourgiant.com

www.ingramcontent.com/pod-product-compliance
Lightning Source LLC
Chambersburg PA
CBHW071332110526
44591CB00010B/1123